MEENA PATHAK CELEBRATES
INDIAN COOKING

MEENA PATHAK CELEBRATES

INDIAN COOKING

100 DELICIOUS RECIPES, 50 YEARS OF PATAK'S

with Anjali Pathak

NEW HOLLAND

Dedication

This book is dedicated to the Founders of Patak's Foods Ltd, my Father-in-law – the late Mr L.G. Pathak, and Mrs Shantagauri Pathak. They were instrumental in having the sheer 'guts' to start making Indian Food 50 years ago in Britain – a country which at that time was relatively new to any foreign food.

The late L.G. Pathak and Mrs S.G. Pathak, 1989

First published in 2007 by
New Holland Publishers (UK) Ltd
London · Cape Town · Sydney · Auckland

Garfield House, 86–88 Edgware Road
London W2 2EA, United Kingdom
www.newhollandpublishers.com

80 McKenzie Street
Cape Town 8001, South Africa

Level 1, Unit 4, 14 Aquatic Drive
Frenchs Forest, NSW 2086, Australia

218 Lake Road, Northcote
Auckland, New Zealand

ISBN 978 1 84537 705 2

SENIOR EDITOR: Clare Sayer
PHOTOGRAPHER: Stuart West
FOOD STYLISTS: Eliza Baird and Vijay Anand
DESIGN: Sue Rose
PRODUCTION: Hazel Kirkman
EDITORIAL DIRECTION: Rosemary Wilkinson

10 9 8 7 6 5 4 3 2 1

Reproduction by Pica Digital PTE Ltd, Singapore
Printed and bound in Malaysia by Times Offset

Contents

6   Introduction

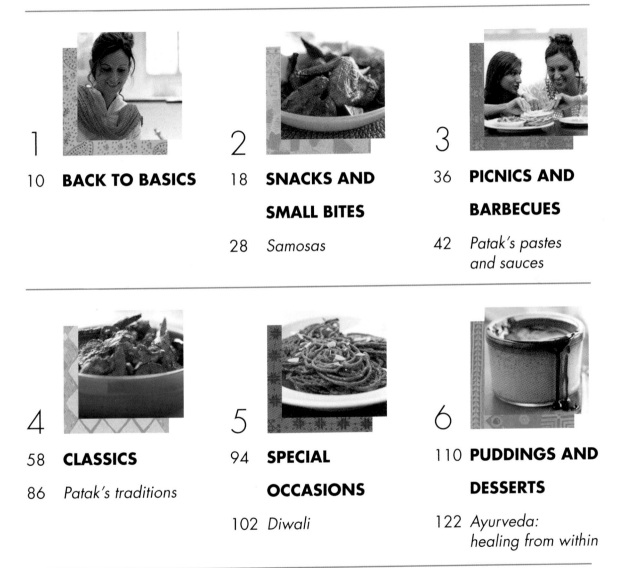

1

10   **BACK TO BASICS**

2

18   **SNACKS AND
     SMALL BITES**

28   *Samosas*

3

36   **PICNICS AND
     BARBECUES**

42   *Patak's pastes
     and sauces*

4

58   **CLASSICS**

86   *Patak's traditions*

5

94   **SPECIAL
     OCCASIONS**

102 *Diwali*

6

110 **PUDDINGS AND
     DESSERTS**

122 *Ayurveda:
     healing from within*

126 Index

128 Acknowledgements

Introduction

Since I wrote my last two cookbooks, I have been inundated with requests for more delicious recipes. This next instalment, as I like to call it, celebrates my husband's heritage: 50 years of Patak's.

The way we cook now is a far cry from how our parents and grandparents cooked 50 years ago. Techniques, ingredients and cooking styles have all developed and Indian food is no different. Clay cooking pots have been replaced with stainless steel saucepans, and those hard-to-find ingredients are now sold at the local shop.

When I was a young girl growing up in Mumbai, my mother used to share with me her experiences as a child, from the food she was brought up on to how she was taught to cook. I now do the same with my daughter, and the changes that have taken place are huge. The recipes in this book reflect these transitional periods, from the basics through to the modern way of cooking. However, the flavour of Indian food has never been lost. It has always been the most exciting cuisine and its use of exotic herbs and spices livens up even the most basic recipes.

Over the last 50 years, Patak's has been a big part of these wonderful changes and is now a household name and an everyday storecupboard item. Whether it is adding a little bit of paste here, or having a bit of chutney there, Patak's influence has been far-reaching. My husband Kirit and I have always tried to make Indian food more accessible and less daunting, for the student who has never cooked, all the way to the experienced chef. My passion has always been to share my knowledge of India and Indian food.

Contents

6   Introduction

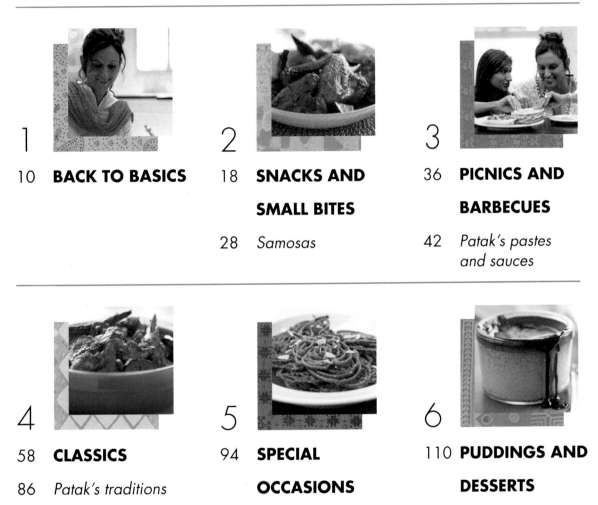

1

10 **BACK TO BASICS**

2

18 **SNACKS AND**
SMALL BITES

28 *Samosas*

3

36 **PICNICS AND**
BARBECUES

42 *Patak's pastes*
and sauces

4

58 **CLASSICS**

86 *Patak's traditions*

5

94 **SPECIAL**
OCCASIONS

102 *Diwali*

6

110 **PUDDINGS AND**
DESSERTS

122 *Ayurveda:*
healing from within

126 Index

128 Acknowledgements

Introduction

Since I wrote my last two cookbooks, I have been inundated with requests for more delicious recipes. This next instalment, as I like to call it, celebrates my husband's heritage: 50 years of Patak's.

The way we cook now is a far cry from how our parents and grandparents cooked 50 years ago. Techniques, ingredients and cooking styles have all developed and Indian food is no different. Clay cooking pots have been replaced with stainless steel saucepans, and those hard-to-find ingredients are now sold at the local shop.

When I was a young girl growing up in Mumbai, my mother used to share with me her experiences as a child, from the food she was brought up on to how she was taught to cook. I now do the same with my daughter, and the changes that have taken place are huge. The recipes in this book reflect these transitional periods, from the basics through to the modern way of cooking. However, the flavour of Indian food has never been lost. It has always been the most exciting cuisine and its use of exotic herbs and spices livens up even the most basic recipes.

Over the last 50 years, Patak's has been a big part of these wonderful changes and is now a household name and an everyday storecupboard item. Whether it is adding a little bit of paste here, or having a bit of chutney there, Patak's influence has been far-reaching. My husband Kirit and I have always tried to make Indian food more accessible and less daunting, for the student who has never cooked, all the way to the experienced chef. My passion has always been to share my knowledge of India and Indian food.

My memories of being introduced to Indian food and traditions are very vivid. In particular I remember the summer I finished my final exams – oh what a relief! It was April and the height of the famous Indian summer had began. Temperatures were soaring into the 40s and the humidity was off the chart. School holidays had begun and plans, as usual, were being made to get away from the sweltering heat. The mango season was in full swing and the female members of the family, children and grandmothers included, had to make the pickles and chutneys for the year ahead. So it was 'all hands on deck' to make sure the task was completed before we all left for the summer. My grandmother was busy ordering the raw green mangoes and my grandfather was getting anxious to book the train tickets to Simla, a Northern Indian town where the climate would be cooler.

We had got word from our vegetable supplier that the best and freshest fruit was being picked off the trees in a village 100 miles from our house in Mumbai, and that we would have it on our doorstep within 48 hours – all 80 kilos of it. My mother, aunt and grandmother began busying themselves with ordering spices, whilst the children were given the task of washing the brass pots and filling them with water ready for the soaking of the fruit. The vegetable wallah kept true to his word and at 7.30 the next morning the doorbell rang. Five men and one woman were standing on the doorstep carrying baskets on their heads full of the freshest mangoes I had ever seen.

Though I was only nine years old, this has become one of my fondest memories. It was a great time to talk about different recipes, but my grandmother was truly in charge. Whenever I asked her the ingredients she would always omit one of them (deliberately). The pickles were made using love and attention, some hot and spicy and some sweet. It was one of my favourite times of the year as it gave us all a chance to exchange family gossip, sing songs and get up to all sorts of pranks. The pickles were made using a secret blend of over eleven different spices known only to my grandmother, which were then tempered in hot oil and mixed with the mangoes. The chutneys were boiled up, whereas the pickles were placed in large earthen pots tied with muslin cloths for maturing. It was then time to unpack our woollen clothes from storage and pack the monstrous tiffin ready for the long journey ahead of us.

This book is all about these memories of learning how to cook as a child. India is a versatile country of colours, spices, flavours, culture and above all, heritage. I have tried to share with you my passion for food and also want to show you how India is evolving constantly. Some of these recipes have been in my family for generations, and I sincerely hope they inspire you to cook.

Fifty years is a milestone for Patak's. My late father-in-law, L.G. as he was fondly known, was the first person to import Indian spices and vegetables into the UK. Even today people remember him as the 'Guru of Indian food' and he is often remembered as a pioneer and ambassador. Kirit can still remember the hardships of 1957 when it all began. Those humble beginnings were the start of something amazing. If I cast my mind back to 1976, when my journey with Patak's began, I realise how fortunate I was to marry into a family that shared my passion for Indian food but I also had something to offer, knowledge. As a girl from Mumbai, having studied Food Technology and being lucky enough to have travelled around visiting my father at various army bases, I had a good solid background to Indian cuisine. When Kirit and I married, I joined the family business and began developing products for them to recreate in their factory. Not an easy task, but 30 years on we are still striving to deliver great tasting authentic recipes. Patak's may have only been around for 50 years but there are so many more years to come. Indian food is evolving all the time and there is so much more to be tasted. We have only begun to show you the diversity within Indian food and we think we might be getting that little bit closer to showing you just what India has to offer. My three grown-up children, Neeraj, Nayan and Anjali, share our passion for Indian food and they are all part of the family business. I am delighted that Anjali has taken a keen interest in cooking – she has even helped me with the recipes in this book. I hope this book stirs excitement and encourages you to learn more about India, its culture and its cuisine. From my kitchen to yours, I hope you are inspired.

Kirit's father (right) in the Drummond Street shop in 1959

BACK to
BASICS

When I was a young girl growing up in India, I learnt a few rules about how to cook an Indian meal. It was daunting cooking with spices for the first time, but some simple steps made it less scary. This chapter is an introduction to cooking with spices and how to use the most basic ingredients to help you create a mouthwatering Indian dish. And at the end of the day, everyone should be able to make a perfect round chapatti and a classic cup of chai.

Basic Indian cooking techniques

Tempering spices

Hot oil has a unique way of releasing the essential aromas and flavours of herbs and spices. Tempering or 'tadka' in Hindi is done at the beginning of a dish or at the final stage of cooking. Tempering is easy and very quick – as long as you remember that you should never add water.

Heat one or two tablespoons of oil in a small pan until very hot and then reduce the heat. Add your whole or ground spices. Remove from the heat when they begin to crackle or change colour.

If this is the final stage of the cooking process then the tadka can be poured straight into lentils or over vegetables or meat. If it is the first stage of cooking then other ingredients can now be added (see below).

Chilli, garlic and ginger paste

Most Indian dishes begin with this basic mixture. Each household will vary the quantities and some of the ingredients may be substituted for their favourite spices. This is made at the weekend in my house, and I use this mix in most of my everyday dishes.

MAKES ABOUT 6 TABLESPOONS

4–5 dried red chillies
3 cloves garlic, peeled
2.5 cm (1 in) fresh root ginger, chopped
1 large bunch fresh coriander (cilantro), stalks and leaves, chopped
3–4 fresh curry leaves
1/2 tablespoon sea salt
1 tablespoon green chilli, chopped

The simplest way to make this paste is to place all the ingredients in a food processor or blender and process to a smooth paste. Add 1–2 tablespoons of water as you blend to achieve a smooth consistency. Store in the refrigerator in an airtight container for up to six days. You can also freeze the paste in ice cube trays.

Sautéed onion sauce base

This simple sauce base can be used for vegetable, meat and fish dishes. Do not be afraid to experiment with your own favourite spice combinations. It will keep for up to five days in an airtight container in the refrigerator.

MAKES ABOUT 450 G (1 LB)
2 tablespoons vegetable oil for frying
1 teaspoon cumin seeds
5 bay leaves (optional)
5 green cardamom pods (optional)
5 cloves (optional)
2 x 2.5 cm (1 in) pieces of cinnamon stick (optional)
1 kg (2 lb 4 oz) onions, peeled and sliced
1 teaspoon salt
25 g (1 oz) butter

In a large pan heat the oil and add the cumin seeds and whole spices. When the spices begin to crackle add the onions and fry on a high heat. Once the onions have turned translucent reduce the heat and allow them to turn golden brown, sprinkling in some water to prevent them from burning. This usually takes about 4–5 minutes. Remove from the heat and take out the large whole spices. Add the salt and butter and stir. Store in an airtight container.

Spiced tomato curry base

This sauce base lends itself particularly well to meat and vegetable dishes.

MAKES ABOUT 450 G (1 LB)
2 tablespoons vegetable oil for frying
1 teaspoon ginger pulp
1 teaspoon garlic pulp
2 green chillies, chopped and deseeded
750 g (1 lb 11oz) fresh tomatoes, chopped
1/2 teaspoon salt
1/2 teaspoon sugar
1/2 teaspoon ground coriander
1/2 teaspoon ground cumin
1/4 teaspoon ground turmeric
1 tablespoon tomato purée
50 g (2 oz) butter

In a large pan heat the oil and add the ginger, garlic and green chillies. Allow to cook for about 5 minutes before adding the tomatoes, salt and sugar. Cook for a further 5 minutes. Add the ground coriander, ground cumin and ground turmeric. Leave to simmer for about 30 minutes. Once the tomatoes have gone mushy and pulpy add the tomato purée and butter. Leave it to simmer for 5 more minutes before removing from the heat. Store in an airtight container.

Roasted spices

Spices really stay fresh for only about four weeks, although in hot weather some lose their flavour more quickly. Ground spices deteriorate even more quickly than whole ones because their essential oils evaporate faster. It is always better, if you can, to buy whole spices and then dry-roast and grind them, as and when you need them. Because I cook for my family every day I grind my spices on a weekend as I have little time during the week. I advise you to only grind a small amount at a time, and try to keep them coarsely ground as they will last a little longer than finely ground spices.

Dry-roasting the spices is essential if you are adding spices after the cooking process has finished. The best spices for this are cumin and coriander. They taste great sprinkled over vegetables and even salads.

MAKES ABOUT 4 TABLESPOONS
3 tablespoons cumin seeds
1 tablespoon coriander seeds

Put the seeds in a heavy-bottomed frying pan and put the pan over a low heat. Keep shaking the pan until the seeds begin to change colour. This happens very quickly so make sure you watch them closely or they will burn. Use a pestle and mortar to crush to your desired consistency.

Keep in an airtight container in a cool dark place.

Meena's garam masala

Every household in India probably has its own special recipe for garam masala, and it tends to be a closely guarded secret handed down through the generations. The basic mixture varies from region to region in India, but the idea of the masala was to heat the body from the inside out. This quantity usually lasts me a few weeks, but you may prefer to make less if you are not cooking Indian food on a daily basis.

150 g (5 oz) cumin seeds
60 g (2½ oz) coriander seeds
50 g (2 oz) green cardamom pods
35 g (1½ oz) black cardamom pods
20 x 2.5 cm (1 in) pieces of cinnamon stick

20 g (³/4 oz) cloves
100 g (4 oz) fennel seeds
15 g (¹/2 oz) bay leaves
2 whole nutmegs

Dry-roast all the spices by putting them in a hot cast-iron frying pan. Stir over a medium heat for 3 minutes or until the mixture starts smoking slightly. Remove from the heat and allow to cool on kitchen paper. Transfer to a coffee or spice grinder and process until you have a fine powder (although I prefer to leave my mixture quite coarse). Store in a dry container with a tight-fitting lid and keep out of direct sunlight. Use within one month.

This masala is great for rounding off the flavour of dishes.

Boiled basmati rice

Rice is one of the main staples of Indian food, particularly in the south, where you are likely to eat rice at every meal. I always recommend using basmati rice, as its aromatic flavour is far superior to other varieties. Its name comes from the Hindi word 'queen of fragrance' and its scent is said to be of the uncluttered freshness of the Himalayan foothills. Cooking rice is really very simple.

SERVES 4
2 cups basmati rice
4 cups water

Wash the basmati rice in several changes of warm water and then allow to soak for 20 minutes. Drain and place the rice in a large pan and cover with four cups of hot water. Bring to the boil, stir gently and then cover. Leave to simmer for 10 minutes until all the water has been absorbed.

Fresh coriander (cilantro) and mint dip

This dip is often eaten with poppadums, koftas and other fried snacks. It has a vibrant green colour, and would be made fresh every day in an Indian household, but you can store it for up to a week in the refrigerator.

150 g (5 oz) fresh coriander (cilantro)
50 g (2 oz) fresh mint
1 green chilli, chopped
4 cloves garlic, crushed
juice of $^1/_2$ lime
250 g (9 oz/4 cups) thick natural yoghurt
$^1/_2$ teaspoon sugar
salt, to taste

Place the fresh coriander (cilantro), fresh mint, green chilli and garlic in a food processor or blender and process to a fine paste. Add the lime juice and a little water if required.

Place the yoghurt in a bowl and whisk in the green paste. Add the sugar and salt.

You can prepare this ahead by freezing the green paste without the yoghurt.

Garlic lover's dip

This dip is a favourite of mine and so quick to make. It always disappears almost before I get a chance to serve it.

4 tablespoons mayonnaise
$^1/_2$ onion, chopped finely
3 cloves garlic, peeled and chopped
1 tablespoon vinegar
1 teaspoon lemon juice
$^1/_2$ teaspoon sugar
salt, to taste
pepper, to taste

Mix all the ingredients together in a glass bowl. Eat with poppadums and anything else you fancy.

TIP Sometimes I make this dip with crème fraîche instead of mayonnaise. A perfect alternative if you are on a diet.

Fruity tamarind and date dip

This dip is often eaten with hot snacks, such as bhajias and samosas. The black salt particularly enhances the flavour.

150 g (5 oz) tamarind pulp
200 g (7 oz) dates
75 g (3 oz/$^1/_3$ cup) brown sugar
4 teaspoons cumin seeds, roasted and ground
$^1/_2$ teaspoon red chilli powder
$^1/_2$ teaspoon black salt (optional)
salt, to taste

Place the tamarind pulp, dates, brown sugar and 400 ml (14 fl oz/1¾ cups) water in a pan and bring to the boil. Cook for 25–30 minutes, stirring occasionally.

Remove from the heat and allow to cool. Place in a food processor or blender and purée to a smooth consistency, making sure there are no seeds in the tamarind pulp. Pass through a sieve.

Add the roasted cumin powder and red chilli powder and black salt, if using. Taste and adjust the seasoning. Store in an airtight container in the refrigerator for up to two weeks.

Indian Flat Bread
Chapatti

Chapattis are eaten all over India as an accompaniment to most meals – they really are a national bread. The art is in the shaping: a good chapatti should be perfectly round and this was one of the first things I learnt to make at home.

MAKES 10

225 g (8 oz/2 cups) chapatti atta flour (wholewheat flour), sieved
½ teaspoon salt (optional)
1 tablespoon vegetable oil
melted ghee or butter

Mix the flour, salt and 150 ml (¼ pint/¼ cup) water in a bowl. Add the oil and knead to a soft dough. Leave covered with a clean damp cloth for 30 minutes.

Knead the dough again for 10 minutes using a little flour to shape it into round balls. Press out each piece on a floured board using your fingers. Roll out with a rolling pin into thin pancakes about 10–12 cm (4–5 in) in diameter.

Heat a flat frying pan or hot griddle. Cook each chapatti over a medium heat for 30 seconds. When one side dries up and tiny bubbles begin to appear, turn over and cook until brown spots appear on the under surface. Press the sides down gently with a clean tea towel.

Remove from the griddle with a pair of tongs and hold directly over the heat/flame until it puffs up. Smear one side with a little ghee or butter and serve immediately.

TIP Chapatti atta flour can be found at all Asian supermarkets.

Indian Puffed Bread
Khasta roti
This superb, soft bread is not eaten as an everyday bread, but more for special occasions. I guarantee it would impress any guests you have round for dinner.

MAKES 6
225 g (8 oz/2 cups) chapatti atta flour (wholewheat flour), sieved
1 teaspoon baking powder
$^1/_2$ teaspoon salt
100 g (4 oz) ghee, melted
1$^1/_2$ teaspoons cumin seeds
100 ml (3$^1/_2$ fl oz/$^1/_2$ cup) milk
2 eggs, beaten

Mix together the flour, baking powder, salt, ghee and cumin seeds in a bowl. Mix well, rubbing the ghee into the flour. Make into a dough by mixing in the milk and the beaten eggs. Set aside, covered, for 20 minutes.

Divide the dough into 6 equal parts and shape into round balls. Roll out each of the rounds into a flat cake about 12 cm (5 in) in diameter.

Cook over a hot griddle for 1 minute on one side and then turn over and cook for a further minute. Continue cooking on both sides, turning frequently until cooked through, about 5–10 minutes. Serve immediately while crispy and hot.

Classic Indian tea
Chai
This spiced tea is served in India every time you ask for tea. Never drunk on its own, it is usually accompanied by bombay mix or fresh hot samosas. Chai is made every morning in my house and my husband Kirit won't leave the house without his daily cup of homemade chai.

SERVES 4
4 teaspoons tea leaves (I prefer Darjeeling but any is fine)
500 ml (18 fl oz/2 cups) whole milk
4–6 teaspoons sugar (optional)
$^1/_4$ teaspoon green cardamom pods, coarsely crushed in a coffee grinder
$^1/_2$ teaspoon ginger pulp
2.5 cm (1 in) piece of cinnamon stick
6–7 mint leaves

Combine all the ingredients together in a large saucepan. Bring to the boil, then reduce the heat and leave to simmer for 2–3 minutes.

Turn off the heat. Cover and allow to rest for 1 minute before straining and serving. Drink piping hot.

TIP If you prefer your tea less milky, use skimmed milk or add more water.

Slumber Coffee
Coffee is said to keep you awake, but this twist on the classic cup of coffee helps you have a lovely night's rest.

SERVES 4
4 teaspoons ground coffee
500 ml (18 fl oz/2 cups) water
400 ml (14 fl oz/1$^3/_4$ cups) skimmed or whole milk
pinch of freshly grated nutmeg
2 x 2.5 cm (1 in) pieces of cinnamon stick
2 green cardamom pods, lightly crushed
25 ml (1 fl oz) Kahlua or any coffee liqueur
4 teaspoons of sugar (optional)

Combine all the ingredients in a large saucepan. Bring to the boil. Reduce the heat and simmer for 2–3 minutes.

Turn off the heat and pass through a strainer. Serve piping hot.

SNACKS
AND
SMALL BITES

Snacking on street food is a huge part of Indian culture. In Mumbai, the streets are always bustling with carts selling all sorts of wonderful delights. One of my fondest childhood memories is of my brother and I sneaking out of the house late at night to the top of our road, where the local street seller was serving the most incredible bhajias. I have never forgotten the taste.

The snacks I've included in this chapter are my absolute favourites. They're great for parties, or even as fillers for the kids after school. And because I've always enjoyed spicing up simple dishes, you'll find things like my Kashmiri chilli chicken wings, which shows how you can give anything a spicy kick.

MEENA'S **chilli ginger mussels**

Seafood is very popular along the coastal regions of India. This delicious recipe makes a mouth-watering treat.

serves four

1 kg (2 lb) mussels (in shell)
1 tablespoon vegetable oil
1 onion, finely chopped
2 cloves garlic, finely chopped
1 cm (1/2 in) fresh root ginger,
  chopped into thin sticks
1 green chilli, chopped
1/2 glass of dry white wine
salt, to taste
2 tablespoons fresh coriander
  (cilantro), chopped

Scrub the mussels well under cold running water and pull out the beards. Make sure you discard any mussels that do not close when tapped with the back of a knife.

In a large pan heat the oil and add the onion. When the onions have turned translucent add the garlic, ginger and green chilli. Turn the heat up and toss in the mussels. Pour in the wine and season with salt. Cover the pan and leave to cook until the shells have opened – about 2 minutes. Then add the coriander (cilantro).

Discard any shells that have not opened. Serve immediately, pouring the juices from the pan over the mussels. Serve with your favourite warm bread. I love eating this with hot naan breads.

spicy chilli FISH CAKES

These wonderful fish cakes are a delicacy of Mumbai, where I grew up. They are a personal favourite.

serves four

50 g (2 oz) butter
50 g (2 oz/1/3 cup) onion, chopped
1/2 teaspoon ground turmeric
2 teaspoons ground coriander
freshly ground black pepper
1 green chilli, chopped
250 g (9 oz) cooked white fish fillets, skins removed
250 g (9 oz/1 1/4 cups) cooked basmati rice
3 eggs
salt, to taste
3 tablespoons fresh coriander (cilantro), chopped
100 g (3 1/2 oz/1 1/2 cups) fresh breadcrumbs
flour for dusting
oil for deep-frying

Melt the butter in a frying pan and add the onion, ground turmeric, ground coriander, black pepper and green chilli. Fry on a low heat for about 5 minutes. Allow to cool.

Place the fish and rice in a food processor or blender and blitz until well combined. Transfer to a large mixing bowl, add the spiced onion mixture, 1 beaten egg, salt and fresh coriander (cilantro). Mix well and divide into 4 equal portions (or 8 smaller portions) and shape into round discs.

Beat the remaining eggs in a shallow dish and place the breadcrumbs and flour on separate sheets of greaseproof paper. Dust the fish cakes with the flour, dip into the egg, and coat with the breadcrumbs, pressing crumbs on lightly.

Heat the oil in a deep-frying pan and fry the fishcakes in batches for about 5 minutes on each side until they are golden brown. Drain well and serve with Fresh coriander (cilantro) and mint dip (see page 15).

East-West BURGERS

This is my version of the all-time British favourite. These were a regular item on the family's menu in the summer months when my children were growing up.

serves six

450 g (1 lb) ground beef

125 g (4 oz) unseasoned dry breadcrumbs

1 1/2 tablespoons natural yoghurt

1 egg, lightly beaten

2 tablespoons Patak's Balti Curry Paste

6 bread rolls, sliced in half

a few handfuls of frisée lettuce

1/2 red onion, sliced into rings

2 tomatoes, sliced into rings

In a bowl combine the beef, breadcrumbs, yoghurt, egg and Patak's Balti Curry Paste. Shape the mixture into six patties and place under a hot grill (broiler) or on a BBQ for 10 minutes, turning occasionally until cooked through.

Assemble the burgers using the bread rolls, lettuce, sliced onion and sliced tomato. I love to add tomato ketchup and mayonnaise before serving.

SPICY STICKY spare ribs

Spare ribs are not really eaten in India, however I have added some spicy ingredients to give this dish an authentic twist.

serves four

4 tablespoons Patak's Madras Curry Paste

1 teaspoon ginger pulp

1 teaspoon garlic pulp

1 tablespoon plain yoghurt

2 tablespoons honey

1 tablespoon lime juice

1 kg (2 lb 4 oz) pork ribs

In a bowl mix together all the ingredients except the ribs. Add the ribs and leave to marinate in the refrigerator for a least 2 hours, overnight would be ideal. Cook in a preheated oven, moderate heat (180°C/350°F/gas 4) for 45 minutes. Check that the ribs are cooked through before placing under a medium grill (broiler) to crisp up.

Serve piping hot.

bay beef SALAD

This is a great way to add a bit of life to a fresh green salad. It tastes fantastic and is low in fat too.

serves four

2 tablespoons Patak's Madras Curry Paste

2 tablespoons fresh coriander (cilantro), chopped

4 beef steaks, battered until thin, fat removed

300 g (11 oz) mixed salad leaves

1/2 red onion, sliced

6 cherry tomatoes, halved

1 tablespoon Greek yoghurt

1/2 cucumber, peeled and finely chopped

1 tablespoon fresh mint, chopped

50 ml (2 fl oz) water

In a bowl mix the Patak's Madras Curry Paste with the coriander (cilantro). Cover the steaks with the marinade. Leave to marinate for 30 minutes, or longer if you have time.

Place the marinated steaks on a hot griddle and leave to cook for 2 minutes before turning over and cooking for a further 2 minutes.

On a large plate mix together the salad leaves, red onion and tomatoes.

In a separate bowl mix the Greek yoghurt with the cucumber and mint and add the water. Stir.

Remove the beef from the griddle and allow to rest.

Slice the beef and lay over the salad leaves. Finally, drizzle over the yoghurt and cucumber dressing and serve.

KASHMIRI **chilli** CHICKEN WINGS

This is one of my old classics that my children used to beg me to make. This shortened version makes it so simple that it can be made a day in advance and cooked through when you need it.

serves four

3 tablespoons Patak's Kashmiri Chilli Sauce

2 teaspoons fresh root ginger, chopped

1 tablespoon honey

juice of 1/2 lime

1/2 teaspoon salt

1 kg (2 lb) chicken wings, raw

In a mixing bowl, throw in all ingredients except the chicken wings. Mix together and then add the wings, rubbing in the marinade well. Cover and leave to marinate in the refrigerator for at least 2 hours or overnight if possible.

Place the marinated wings on a non-stick baking sheet and place in an oven preheated to a moderate heat (180°/350°F/gas 4) for 25 minutes, turning half way through cooking. If you like your wings crispy, turn the grill (broiler) on 5 minutes before the end of cooking and watch the skins turn golden brown.

tikka POTATO WEDGES AND DIP

These potato wedges are great to serve at a party or as a light snack, but they also make a wonderful alternative to roast potatoes. Originally from the western coasts of India, it has become a family favourite.

serves eight

- **1 kg (2 lb) potatoes**
- **4 tablespoons vegetable oil**
- **1 tablespoon plain (all-purpose) flour**
- **4 tablespoons Patak's Tikka Masala Curry Paste**
- **2 tablespoons soured cream**
- **1/2 tablespoon chives, chopped**
- **1 teaspoon lemon juice**
- **1/4 teaspoon ground paprika**

Cut the potatoes into wedges and boil until they are just cooked through but still firm. Drain.

In an ovenproof dish mix the oil, flour and Patak's Tikka Masala Curry Paste together, making sure there are no lumps. Toss the potatoes into the dish and shake around so all wedges are coated with the Tikka marinade. Roast in a moderate oven (180°C/350°F/gas 4) for about 35 minutes, or until golden brown and crispy.

In bowl mix the soured cream, chives, lemon juice and paprika together. Serve alongside the potato wedges for a tasty snack.

IRRESISTIBLE spiced beans on toast

This is a great snack to have when you have come home from a long day at work and don't feel like doing any cooking.

serves two

- **1 teaspoon vegetable oil**
- **1 teaspoon cumin seeds**
- **1 green chilli, seeded and chopped**
- **pinch of asafoetida**
- **400 g (14 oz) can of baked beans**
- **2 slices of bread**
- **1 tablespoon grated cheese**
- **1 teaspoon fresh coriander (cilantro), chopped**
- **1 tablespoon chopped onions**

Heat the oil and add the cumin seeds. When they begin to crackle add the green chilli and asafoetida. After 30 seconds add the baked beans. Give the mixture a good stir, then reduce the heat.

Toast the bread under the grill (broiler) or in a toaster. When the baked beans are heated through tip them onto each piece of toast. Sprinkle the grated cheese, coriander (cilantro) and onions over the beans.

Place under a preheated grill and cook briefly until the cheese begins to melt and brown. Serve at once.

Tikka potato wedges and dip

SAMOSAS

Now famous the world over, you'll find these distinctive, triangular deep-fried snacks throughout India with all sorts of weird and wonderful fillings, from spiced potatoes and peas, to minced lamb and onions. Perfect with a piping hot chai, they're cheap, tasty and sold everywhere. Street vendors even carry them around in baskets attached to their waists or balanced on their heads.

The size of a samosa and the consistency of the pastry can vary from region to region, but the best way to guess where they originate from is from the spicing. In the north, you're likely to find nuts and plenty of fresh coriander (cilantro) and cumin seeds. In the south, you'll find a hotter blend of spices, with ground coriander, curry leaves and lots of fresh green chillies. But whatever the filling, any fresh hot samosa is delicious dipped in mango chutney and coriander (cilantro) and mint dip.

Samosas were one of the first things my late father-in-law made and sold when he moved to England with his family. He began selling them to local Indian students in London, but as word spread, demand grew big enough for him to open up a small shop in Kentish Town, where hundreds were made and sold every day. His family,

including Kirit, my then husband-to-be, started to help and Patak's was born. To this day, the samosa recipe has remained true and original, so it's as good now as it was then.

There's nothing better than fresh homemade samosas. When Kirit was a schoolboy, his mother used to pack fresh samosas away in his lunchbox. She liked to call it a taste from home, and when I make my vegetarian samosas, I do the same and pack some up for my children to take home with them. My daughter Anjali likes to make her samosas with a filling of chocolate and nuts, and although not a common Indian recipe, there's nothing wrong with making something Indian with a twist.

Ever since I was a child, I've loved samosas. I always will. I hope they are – or become – a favourite of yours too.

TIP

I use filo pastry as it is easier to use and, because it is lighter, it doesn't soak up as much oil. Keep the filo pastry sheet covered with a damp cloth while you are working to prevent it drying out.

FRESH VEGETABLE samosas

These deep-fried snacks are eaten all over India. The fillings vary from region to region, stuffed with meat in the south and vegetables in the north. When eaten during Diwali they are often stuffed with sweet fillings. My children used to love making these with me when they were young.

makes 16

250 g (9 oz/1¼ cups) potatoes, peeled and cut into chunks
100 g (4 oz/¾ cup) peas, thawed (if frozen)
3 tablespoons oil or ghee
1½ teaspoons coriander seeds, crushed
15 g (½ oz) fresh root ginger, chopped
5 cloves garlic, chopped
1 green chilli, chopped
2 teaspoons ground coriander
¾ teaspoon ground cumin
½ teaspoon ground fennel
⅛ teaspoon ground black pepper
pinch of salt
4 tablespoons fresh coriander (cilantro), chopped
16 sheets filo pastry, each 8 x 20 cm (3 x 8 in) (see Tip)
flour and water for sealing
vegetable oil for deep-frying

Bring a large pan of salted water to the boil, add the potatoes to the pan and cook for 15–20 minutes until soft. Drain and allow to cool.

Cook the peas in boiling water for 5 minutes, drain and set aside. Roughly mash the potatoes and mix with the peas.

Heat the 3 tablespoons of oil or ghee in a large pan and add the crushed coriander seeds. When they begin to crackle, add the ginger, garlic and green chilli. Fry for 2 minutes. Add the ground spices, sprinkle with water and fry for 3–4 minutes on low heat. Pour the mixture over the potatoes and peas and mix well. Add the salt and chopped fresh coriander (cilantro).

Take a piece of filo pastry and make the first diagonal fold, then the second and the third (see below).

Open up the pouch and use a teaspoon to fill the samosa, making sure you don't overfill it or it will burst in the frying pan. Make a paste with the flour and water and smear the remaining flap. Close and press to 'glue' the opening and seal the filling in. Repeat this process for each samosa.

Deep-fry a few samosas at a time in hot oil at 190°C (375°F) for 5–10 minutes. Remove from the oil with a slotted spoon and leave to drain on absorbent kitchen paper. Serve warm with Fresh coriander (cilantro) and mint dip or Tamarind and date dip (see page 15).

SPICED **cashews**

These are great to eat on a summer's evening whilst out in the garden chatting with friends.

serves four

¹/₂ teaspoon salt
1 teaspoon brown sugar
¹/₂ teaspoon red chilli powder
juice of ¹/₂ lime
100 g (3¹/₂ oz) unsalted cashews

Mix together all the ingredients, except the cashews, in a bowl. Add the nuts to the mixture and try to make sure all are coated evenly. Lay out the cashews on a non-stick baking sheet and cook in a preheated oven at a moderate heat (200°C/400°F/gas 6) for 10 minutes. When the cashews are golden brown and the sugar has caramelized, tip out into a bowl. Allow to cool slightly before serving.

Caramelised ONION BHAJIAS

Another favourite amongst my family and eaten all over India, these snacks are easy to make and any leftovers can be chopped up and added as an alternative to croutons in a fresh salad. They also taste great dipped into Fresh coriander (cilantro) and mint dip (see page 15).

Serves four to six

300 g (11 oz) chickpea (gram) flour
1 teaspoon garlic pulp
¹/₂ teaspoon ground turmeric
³/₄ teaspoon red chilli powder
salt, to taste
¹/₄ teaspoon asafoetida
400 g (14 oz/3 cups) red onions, sliced lengthways
2 tablespoons fresh coriander (cilantro), chopped
oil for deep-frying

Mix together the chickpea flour, 50–75 ml (2–3 fl oz) water, garlic, ground turmeric, red chilli powder, salt and asafoetida to form a thick paste.

Add the sliced red onions and chopped coriander (cilantro) and mix well. Take small handfuls of the onion batter and deep-fry in batches in oil over a medium heat for 10–15 minutes until they turn golden brown and the bhajias are cooked through. Remove with a slotted spoon and drain on absorbent kitchen paper. Serve hot.

MEENA'S **corn-on-the-cob**

Bhutta

This is one of my Sunday favourites but it is always good as snack – any time you want!

serves two

2 sweetcorn cobs, husks removed

**1 tablespoon fresh coriander
   (cilantro), chopped**

2 teaspoons butter

1/4 teaspoon red chilli powder

juice of 1/2 lemon

salt, to taste

Fill a pan with water and boil the corn until tender, about 10 minutes.

   Mix together the coriander (cilantro), butter, chilli and lemon juice and brush over the sweetcorn. Season with salt and serve piping hot.

the anytime INDIAN OMELETTE

My husband Kirit has to have everything with a little spice, even his breakfast foods. This quick omelette will kick-start anyone's morning.

serves two

2 tablespoons vegetable oil

1 green chilli, chopped

**1 teaspoon fresh root ginger,
   chopped**

1 red onion, sliced

4 eggs, beaten

**1 tomato, seeds removed and
   chopped**

1/4 teaspoon salt

**1/4 teaspoon black pepper,
   coarsely ground**

**1 tablespoon fresh coriander
   (cilantro), chopped**

In a shallow frying pan heat the oil and add the chilli, ginger and onion. Fry for 3 minutes. Remove half the mixture and set aside (this is for the remaining omelette).

   In a bowl mix the remaining ingredients together. Pour half of the egg mixture into the frying pan and shake around so the egg mixture coats the bottom of the pan.

   Fry for 2 minutes fluffing up the omelette as it cooks. If desired turn over and leave to cook, or if you prefer your omelette runny remove from the heat. Repeat with the rest of the ingredients to make a second omelette. Serve immediately with warm bread and tomato ketchup.

CHICKEN **and lentil broth**

A popular dish eaten in the winter months as it can get quite cool in the north of India. I prefer to use chicken bones in this dish as it gives good flavour, but 1¹/₂ litres (2¹/₂ pints) of chicken stock is fine.

Serves six to eight

2 kg (4¹/₂ lbs) raw chicken bones
500 g (1¹/₄ lbs/4¹/₂ cups)
  onions, sliced
1 tablespoon garlic pulp
4 teaspoons ginger pulp
³/₄ teaspoon ground turmeric
1 tablespoon ground coriander
1 teaspoon ground fennel
1¹/₂ teaspoons ground cumin
8 cardamom pods
5 bay leaves
8 cloves
400 g (14 oz) can chopped
  tomatoes
75 g (3 oz) fresh coriander
  (cilantro)
2 tablespoons vegetable oil
75 g (3 oz) chickpea (gram) flour
  or ground lentils
¹/₂ teaspoon salt
juice of ¹/₂ lemon
50 g (2 oz) fresh mint, chopped
finely diced poached chicken, to
  garnish

First make the stock. Place the chicken bones in a large, heavy-based saucepan and cover with cold water. Add all the ingredients except the oil, chickpea flour, salt, lemon juice, mint leaves and diced chicken and bring to the boil. Simmer for 3–4 hours until the water is reduced to one-third of its original quantity. Strain the stock through a fine sieve or muslin cloth and put into another pan to boil.

In a separate pan combine the oil and chickpea flour and cook, stirring, for 2–3 minutes on a low heat. When the chickpea flour begins to bubble add the mixture to the strained chicken stock and bring to the boil, ensuring that no lumps form and the stock becomes slightly thicker in consistency. Add the salt and lemon juice. Serve garnished with the fresh mint and diced chicken.

POTATOES **stuffed with** GREEN PEAS

Aloo tikkis

You will probably have seen these little treats appearing on Indian menus. They taste great dipped into Fresh coriander (cilantro) and mint dip (see page 15) or simply on their own.

serves four as a snack

500 g (1 lb/3 cups) potatoes, peeled and cut into 2.5 cm (1 in) cubes

salt, to taste

cornflour (cornstarch), for binding

200 g (7 oz/1¹/₃ cups) green peas, thawed (if frozen) and cooked

vegetable oil for shallow frying

1 teaspoon cumin seeds

1 teaspoon fresh root ginger, chopped

¹/₂ teaspoon green chillies, chopped

¹/₂ teaspoon cumin seeds, roasted and ground (see page 13)

¹/₄ teaspoon ground turmeric

¹/₄ teaspoon ground coriander

squeeze of lemon juice

1 teaspoon fresh coriander (cilantro), chopped

Boil the potatoes in water until they are cooked through. Drain off any excess water and mash them until very smooth. Season with salt and add a little cornflour (cornstarch) for binding.

Squeeze out all the moisture from the green peas and set aside.

Heat half the oil in a frying pan and add the cumin seeds. When they begin to crackle add the ginger and green chillies. Add the green peas, roasted cumin, ground turmeric and ground coriander. Stir and fry until the mixture has dried out. Add lemon juice, fresh coriander (cilantro) leaves and season with salt. Leave the mixture to cool.

Take about 50 g (2 oz) of mashed potato mixture and soften in your hands, then stuff with 25 g (1 oz) of the green pea mixture. Make a smooth ball by closing the mash around the peas. Flatten gently to form a small round disc.

Heat some oil in a pan and shallow fry the tikkis, turning occasionally until golden brown. Drain on absorbent paper.

TIP
Making the tikkis into discs can be quite tricky, so sometimes I find it easier to pat them with a little flour before shaping.

PICNICS
and barbecues

My favourite time of year has to be summertime so I had to include this chapter full of food perfect for eating outside, whether barbecued or cooked at home and packed away for a picnic. And because I always like to cook a variety of dishes when entertaining, I've included a range of recipes, from traditional Indian, such as my Seekh kebabs, to ones with an Indian twist, like Tandoori chicken caesar salad.

BOMBAY **pitta pockets**

This recipe takes me back to my school days, when we used to eat these on our first break between classes. This is great for taking on a picnic.

serves four

4 small pitta breads

butter, for spreading

8 tablespoons Fresh coriander and mint dip (see page 15)

1 potato, boiled, peeled and sliced into rounds

3 tomatoes, sliced

1 red onion, sliced into rings

16 slices of cucumber

salt and pepper, to taste

Lightly toast the pitta breads or warm them in the oven so you can open them up easily. Spread the insides lightly with butter and then spread 1 tablespoon of the coriander (cilantro) and mint dip over each side. Fill the pitta pockets with sliced potato, tomatoes, onion and cucumber. Sprinkle with salt and pepper. Serve with a crisp green salad.

seared KERALAN PRAWNS

This recipe brings back memories of my childhood, when we would holiday in the South of India. The lush green coastal state of Kerala always had mouthwatering seafood dishes on offer. This particular dish is a quick version of a traditional recipe.

serves four

2 tablespoons Patak's Korma Curry Paste

1 tablespoon natural yoghurt

1 teaspoon olive oil

32 jumbo prawns (shrimp), with tails

8 wooden skewers, soaked in water for half an hour

1 teaspoon desiccated coconut

In a bowl mix the Patak's Korma Curry Paste and yoghurt together. Add the olive oil and prawns (shrimp). Leave to marinate for about 30 minutes or so and thread onto the skewers.

Place on the BBQ or under a hot grill and cook for 5 minutes, or until the prawns (shrimp) are cooked through.

Sprinkle over some desiccated coconut and serve with a fresh homemade dip (see page 15).

CHILLI CHICKEN **wrap**

Wraps are great to eat at any time of the day. In India they are filled with all sorts of wonderful ingredients, vegetarian and non-vegetarian.

serves four
- **2 chicken breasts, skin removed and cut into strips**
- **4 tablespoons Patak's Kashmiri Chilli Sauce**
- **4 flour tortillas or wraps**
- **50 g (2 oz) lettuce, shredded**
- **75 g (3 oz) cucumber, sliced**
- **1 red onion, sliced**
- **1 tablespoon fresh coriander (cilantro), chopped**
- **salt and pepper, to taste**

In a bowl marinate the chicken breast strips with half the Patak's Kashmiri Chilli Sauce for about 30 minutes. Cook the chicken under a moderate grill (broiler) for 15 minutes, or on a skillet for 10 minutes. Check the chicken is cooked before removing and setting aside.

Lay out the tortillas and spoon the remaining Patak's Kashmiri Chilli Sauce down the centre of each wrap. Sprinkle each with lettuce, cucumber and red onion.

Divide the chicken strips amongst the wraps. Sprinkle with fresh coriander (cilantro) and season with salt and pepper. Roll up the wraps and serve with a fresh green salad.

the ultimate snack WITH CACHUMBAR

A picnic would not be the same without this great tasting snack to munch on.

serves four
- **2 green chillies**
- **250 g (9 oz) red onions**
- **150 g (5 oz) firm red tomatoes**
- **100 g (3 1/2 oz) cucumber**
- **2 tablespoons fresh coriander (cilantro), chopped**
- **juice of 1 lime**
- **1 teaspoon black mustard seeds, coarsely crushed**
- **1 teaspoon sugar**
- **salt, to taste**
- **8 ready-cooked poppadums**

Chop the green chillies, seeding them first to reduce the heat if you prefer. Peel and chop the onions, chop the tomatoes and peel and dice the cucumber.

Combine all the ingredients together, except the poppadums, and mix well. If possible, cover and leave at room temperature for at least 15 minutes so the flavours have time to develop.

When you are ready to serve just place the Cachumbar in a bowl and eat by scooping onto the poppadums.

CHARGRILLED **steak** SANDWICH

Another barbecue favourite – I always receive compliments on it whenever it is cooked.

serves four

3 tablespoons Patak's Balti Curry Paste

2 tablespoons natural set yoghurt

4 steaks, about 175 g (6 oz) each

4 crusty baguettes, sliced lengthways

100g (3¹/₂ oz) rocket (arugula) leaves

1 tablespoon fresh coriander (cilantro), chopped

4 tablespoons Patak's Raita

In a bowl mix the Patak's Balti Curry Paste with the yoghurt. Rub the marinade well into the steaks and place in the refrigerator for about an hour.

Shake off any excess marinade from the steaks and place directly onto the barbecue. Turn them after 3–4 minutes and continue cooking. Alternatively, cook under a moderate grill (broiler) for about 7 minutes, turning once.

In the meantime prepare the bread: slice the baguettes and divide the rocket (arugula) leaves between them.

Remove the steaks from the barbecue and leave to rest for a few minutes before placing in the baguettes. Sprinkle with fresh coriander (cilantro), spoon over Patak's Raita and serve hot.

PATAK'S PASTES
and **sauces**

The Patak's range is always expanding to include new products

I have often been credited for creating the ready-to-use curry pastes that you see on the shelves today. This amazing invention was actually the brainchild of my late father-in-law and was developed in the early 60s.

It was prompted by the demand for good home cooking from the Indian students who were busy getting their law or medical degrees from universities in and around London. They used to frequent the shop in Drummond Street near Euston Station and they would buy all their Indian groceries from pickles through to spices. The only problem for them was that they did not know how to cook from scratch. They pleaded with him to make life easier for them and help them get the home cooking they longed for. My father-in-law saw this as an opportunity not to be missed and began experimenting in his kitchen after work. After all, what was he going to do with the spices on his shelves if the students weren't buying them anymore? As he experimented he began getting closer to what was to be the first curry paste the world had ever seen. First he ground the spices in small quantities, crushed the ginger, garlic, chillies and coriander (cilantro) leaves, and then gently stir-fried them and put them into little jars with a little oil. He then tested them out by letting the students try them at home with little instructions on how to use it scribbled on a piece of paper.

A week later they returned and said that it was good but there was something missing. It was back to the kitchen for more experimenting, but it wasn't long before the recipe had been perfected and the 'Mild Curry Paste' was born.

This was the beginning of a new revolution for Indian cooks, a kitchen ingredient that made life simpler. The very young Kirit Pathak knew that this was the future if Indian food was to become popular within the UK and worldwide, and so had great aspirations for a range of curry pastes. It was at this time that I married into the family and unbeknown to them I had qualified with a food technology degree back in India. Kirit and my father-in-law (or Bapuji as we respectfully called him) wanted to test my skills in the kitchen and so gave me the challenge of creating a paste for a universally recognised Indian flavour – 'Tandoori'. Looking back now I can see how they were trying to trick me and I am sure they never imagined that I would create a product which we still sell today. Nonetheless, I got to work on the recipe development in our family kitchen. The other family members would often wander in and

I would find myself having to hide my inventions so that the surprise would not be ruined: a trait I learnt from my secretive grandmother.

After much hard work I was ready. The true test was upon me and it was time to prove myself to my new family. Bapuji tasted it first and said nothing, but as I soon found out, he was a man that could never hide his emotions. Kirit tasted it next and immediately I could see a smile forming. They both loved it. I was relieved, but they couldn't be happier as they had found their new head of recipe development.

This was the start of many inventions and over the last 50 years we have created more curry pastes, each one packed with authentic flavours.

The next stepping stone was to be cooking sauces people could use at home. So once again I put on my creative hat and it was an overnight thought process which brought about the launch of the 'Sauce in Glass' era. I was so dedicated and passionate about this idea that I consciously shut myself off from everyone while the idea was still buzzing in my head.

Experiments began and I was busy thinking about flavours, authenticity, regional spice combinations, but above all, whether cooks would understand this new invention of mine.

I spoke to Kirit and the marketing team at Patak's about my idea and I could tell they were sceptical. They had varied opinions but I did not let that dampen my enthusiasm so I carried on. I was convinced that this would work and within a matter of two weeks I had created basic flavours that I was ready to present to the team.

I was nervous on the day of presentation yet silently confident that making life easier for the lover of Indian food was just around the corner. I knew my invention would eventually work – and it did! I got an astounding positive response and we soon began making Indian sauces and selling them to supermarkets.

Even today I find it quite amusing to remember the quizzical expressions on the faces of Kirit and the tasting panel. I still continue creating new pastes and new eating experiences and I doubt I will ever stop. I will never forget the first paste I created for the brand in 1977 and the range of sauces I first developed in 1990.

Thirty years on they both exist side by side on supermarket shelves all over the world.

An original Patak's label from the 1960s

CHICKEN TIKKA **caesar salad**

This is a great fusion dish that I invented over 20 years ago. I am always thinking up new ways to add some Indian flair to everyday favourites.

serves four

2 tablespoons Patak's Tikka Masala Curry Paste

2 tablespoons plain yoghurt

4 skinless chicken breasts

1 garlic and coriander (cilantro) naan

2 tablespoons Patak's Raita

1/4 teaspoon black pepper, coarsely ground

1 tablespoon fresh coriander (cilantro), chopped

2 tablespoons water

2 romaine or cos lettuces

fresh Parmesan cheese to garnish (optional)

In a bowl mix the Patak's Tikka Masala Curry Paste with the plain yoghurt. Add the chicken and coat well with the marinade. Cover and refrigerate for at least 2 hours. Cook under a moderate grill (broiler) or on the barbecue for 20 minutes until the chicken is cooked through, basting with the extra marinade as it cooks. Set aside and leave to cool.

Place the naan under a medium grill (broiler) for a few minutes until lightly toasted. Cut into cubes.

In another bowl mix Patak's Raita with the black pepper and add the coriander (cilantro). Add the water and mix.

Place the lettuce leaves in a large bowl and toss with half the dressing. Arrange on a serving dish.

Slice the chicken into strips and lay on top of the salad leaves. Sprinkle over the naan bread cubes and drizzle over the remaining dressing. Serve with freshly shaved Parmesan cheese.

mini STUFFED JACKETS

Hot jacket potatoes have always been a comfort food of mine and I am always thinking of new ways to spice them up. This is an easy recipe that livens up the simplest of foods.

serves four

150 g (5 oz) baby new potatoes

1 tablespoon olive oil

1 tablespoon Patak's Madras Curry Paste

2 tablespoons cream cheese or soured cream

chopped chives, to garnish

TIP
If you prefer, you can bake the potatoes in a preheated oven on a moderate heat (180°C/350°F/gas 4) for about 45 minutes.

Scrub the new potatoes to remove any dirt. Prick them with a fork to prevent the skins from bursting.

Grease a piece of foil with the olive oil, and toss the potatoes in, closing all the sides to make a parcel. Place them on the barbecue and cook for 30 minutes.

In the meantime you can make the stuffing. Place the Patak's Madras Curry Paste in a pan with about 2 tablespoons of water. Place on a medium heat. When the oil begins to separate from the mixture remove from the heat and leave to cool.

Once the mixture has cooled place in a bowl and mix with the cream cheese.

When the potatoes are cooked through remove from the barbecue. Cut a cross in the centre of each potato and stuff the potatoes with the cream cheese mixture.

Garnish with chopped chives and serve hot.

short-eats

India loves to snack. Whenever I travel back the first thing I see is the street wallahs selling all sorts of weird and wonderful foods. They call these vegetable snacks short-eats. They are packed full of nutritional goodness. This dip is not traditionally Indian but tastes great with this recipe.

Serves four as a snack

1 cucumber, cut into thin sticks

3 carrots, peeled and cut into thin sticks

3 celery sticks, tops removed and cut into thin sticks

3 tablespoons soured cream

2 tablespoons chives, chopped finely

1 teaspoon lemon juice

salt to taste

1/2 teaspoon ground paprika

On a plate lay the cucumber, carrots and celery.

In a bowl mix together the soured cream, chives, lemon juice, pinch of salt and paprika powder.

Serve with the crudités.

MANGO-GLAZED pork chops

This dish is so easy to make and you can marinade the chops the night before.

serves four

3 tablespoons Patak's Sweet Mango Chutney

1 tablespoon vegetable oil

2 teaspoons fresh root ginger, grated

salt and freshly cracked black pepper

4 large pork chops

Patak's Sweet Mango Chutney, to serve

In a bowl mix together all the ingredients, except the pork chops. Season with salt and pepper and add the chops, coating them in the marinade. Cover, place in the refrigerator and leave to marinate for a least 2 hours, preferably overnight.

Place on the barbecue, or in a preheated oven, moderate heat (180°C/350°F/gas 4) for about 20 minutes. Brush with the excess marinade regularly. Serve hot with extra Patak's Sweet Mango Chutney for dipping.

TIP

You can add more mango chutney for a more intense flavour.

ROASTED TIKKA **vegetable panini**

Most of the population of India is vegetarian, and the choice of vegetable dishes is huge. This is a great way to cater for your vegetarian guests without them feeling that they are missing out.

serves four

2 tablespoons olive oil

1 tablespoon Patak's Tikka Masala Curry Paste

1/2 teaspoon mixed herbs

1 tablespoon capers, rinsed (if soaked in brine)

1 tablespoon green or black olives, sliced

1 yellow (bell) pepper, sliced

1 medium red onion, sliced

50 g (2 oz) fine green beans, halved

50 g (2 oz) asparagus tips, halved

cracked black pepper for seasoning

4 panini rolls, sliced in half

100 g (3 1/2 oz) mozzarella cheese, sliced

In a large oven dish mix the olive oil and Patak's Tikka Masala Curry Paste. Sprinkle in the herbs, capers and olives. Add the vegetables and mix thoroughly, ensuring all vegetables are covered in the marinade. Season with cracked black pepper. Bake in a moderate oven (180°C/350°F/gas 4) for 25–30 minutes.

Remove from the oven and place the vegetables on the panini rolls, before adding the sliced mozzarella. Place in a panini sandwich maker and cook following the manufacturer's instructions. Serve piping hot.

TIP

If you are cooking this on the barbecue, instead of placing the vegetables in the oven simply wrap them in foil and cook on the barbecue.

tandoori crusted SALMON

One of the first pastes I ever created was a classic tandoori paste, which we still sell today. This is a wonderful dish, perfect for cooking on a summer's evening.

serves four

1 1/2 tablespoons Patak's Tandoori Curry Paste

50 g (2 oz/1 cup) fresh breadcrumbs

25 g (1 oz/1/3 cup) oats

2 tablespoons fresh parsley, chopped

1/2 teaspoon lemon zest

4 salmon fillets (about 90 g / 3 1/2 oz each)

juice of 1 lime

In a bowl mix together the Patak's Tandoori Curry Paste, breadcrumbs, oats, parsley and lemon zest.

If you are cooking it in the oven, lay the salmon fillets on a non-stick baking sheet and coat with the crust mixture, patting down lightly. Bake in a preheated oven, at 200°C/400°F/gas 6 for 10 minutes. Remove, cover with foil and then bake for a further 10 minutes.

If you are cooking on the barbecue, grease four pieces of foil (20 x 20 cm/8 x 8 in) and lay a salmon fillet in the centre of each one. Fold up the edges and cook on the barbecue for 20 minutes.

Once the tandoori salmon is cooked, squeeze over the lime juice. Serve with a crunchy salad and garnish with lime wedges.

SMOKY **sweet potatoes**

This is a very simple recipe that has lovely hints of the aromatic spices. It is great as an accompaniment to barbecues.

serves four
900 g (2 lbs) sweet potatoes
2 cloves garlic, crushed
**2 tablespoons cumin seeds,
  roasted and ground (see
  page 13)**
2 tablespoons olive oil
juice of 1 lemon
cracked black pepper, to taste
salt, to taste

Scrub the sweet potatoes and cut them into bite-size pieces.

In a large bowl mix together the remaining ingredients. Add the potatoes to the bowl and toss them in the mixture, coating them evenly. Transfer to a baking sheet and roast in a preheated oven at 180°C/350°F/gas 4 for about 15 minutes.

Move the potatoes around every five minutes so that they brown on all sides. Remove from the oven once cooked or when you can easily pierce with a fork. Serve hot with a fresh raita.

spicy LAMB **kebabs**
Seekh kebabs

This is a barbecue favourite of my children. Papaya is a great meat tenderiser.

serves four
450 g (1 lb) ground lamb
100 g (4 oz) onions, sliced
4 teaspoons ginger pulp
1 tablespoon garlic pulp
**3 tablespoons fresh coriander
  (cilantro), chopped**
**3 tablespoons fresh mint,
  chopped**
1 teaspoon garam masala
3/4 teaspoon red chilli powder
1/2 teaspoon ground turmeric
25 g (1 oz) fresh papaya
salt, to taste
50 g (2 oz) butter, melted

Mix all the ingredients together except the butter. Place in a food processor or blender and process until you have a coarse paste. Mix in half the melted butter.

Take a handful of the mixture and wrap it around a skewer to form a sausage shape about 10 cm (4 in) long and 2.5 cm (1 in) in diameter. Roll in your hands to ensure the meat is firmly compressed around the skewer. Repeat with the remaining mixture to make 8 kebabs.

Cook over charcoal or under a hot grill (broiler) for about 10 minutes. Remove from the skewer and smear with the remaining melted butter and serve hot with a fresh tomato and onion salad.

SOUTH INDIAN
steamed monkfish parcels

Traditionally the fish in this recipe is steamed in a banana leaf. However, I have modified it for you to make it easier. I recommend serving the fish wrapped in the parcel so that your guests can smell the beautiful aroma once the parcels are ripped open.

serves four

200 g (7 oz) desiccated coconut

75 g (3 oz) fresh coriander (cilantro), roughly chopped

25 g (1 oz) fresh mint leaves

2 tablespoons natural yoghurt

6 cloves garlic

1 teaspoon black mustard seeds

50 ml (2 fl oz) lemon juice

2 teaspoons sugar

salt, to taste

2 tablespoons vegetable oil

20 curry leaves, plus a few extra for garnish

4 monkfish fillets, or other white fleshy fish such as cod

Cut 4 pieces of foil into squares, about 20 cm x 20 cm (8 in x 8 in).

In a food processor or blender, combine the desiccated coconut, coriander (cilantro), mint, yoghurt, garlic and mustard seeds. Add a little water to help make a fine paste. Then add the lemon juice and sugar, and check the salt.

Heat the oil in a pan and add the curry leaves. After about a minute, remove from the pan and set aside.

Spread a little of the green paste onto each square of foil and place a monkfish fillet on top. Spread a little more paste on top of the fish and then add the tempered curry leaves. Carefully wrap and seal the parcels making sure that no paste can escape.

Place on a barbecue, or into a preheated oven (180°C/350°F/gas 4) for 25 minutes.

Check that the fish is cooked through before serving hot with some steamed rice. Garnish with fried curry leaves.

TANDOORI CHICKEN **summer salad**

Tandoori chicken and summer go superbly together. This is a crunchy salad that always features on my list whenever I cook for friends in the summer. It tastes great hot or cold so you can make it a day in advance to save time.

serves four

2 tablespoons Patak's Tandoori Curry Paste

2 tablespoons plain yoghurt

4 skinless chicken breasts

200 g (7 oz) green beans

500 g (1 lb 2 oz) beansprouts

150 g (5 oz) cherry tomatoes, halved

50 g (2 oz) baby spinach leaves

100 g (4 oz/3/4 cup) unsalted roasted peanuts

1/2 red onion, finely sliced, to garnish

DRESSING

2 tablespoons sesame seeds

1 tablespoon extra virgin olive oil

juice of 1/2 lime

3 tablespoons Patak's Tangy Fruit (tamarind and date) Sauce

2 tablespoons Patak's Kashmiri Chilli Sauce

2 tablespoons fresh coriander (cilantro), chopped

salt and pepper, to taste

In a bowl mix Patak's Tandoori Curry Paste and yoghurt together. Add the chicken breasts and coat with the mixture. Cover and leave to marinate in the refrigerator for at least 2 hours.

Under a moderate grill (broiler), cook the chicken for about 20 minutes or until cooked through, basting with the excess marinade during cooking. Leave to rest.

Bring a large saucepan of salted water to the boil. Blanch the green beans for 1 minute and remove with a slotted spoon, leaving to drain.

To make the dressing, toast the sesame seeds in a dry frying pan for 1 minute until they turn light golden brown. Place in a bowl and add the olive oil, lime juice, Patak's Tangy Fruit Sauce, Patak's Kashmiri Chilli Sauce, coriander and season with salt and pepper. Mix well.

Cut the chicken into slices and place in a large bowl. Add the beansprouts, cherry tomatoes, baby spinach, green beans, peanuts and red onion. Pour the dressing over and toss the salad. Serve warm or cold.

GRILLED **aromatic fruits**

This is a healthy snack, and a great way to get children to eat their fruit.

Serves six to eight

**wooden skewers, soaked in
    water for 30 minutes**
1 pineapple
**200 g (7 oz) strawberries, stalks
    removed, cut in half lengthways**
**1 green apple, core removed and
    cut into large cubes**
¹/4 teaspoon sugar
¹/2 teaspoon ground cinnamon
**1 teaspoon cumin seeds, roasted
    and ground (see page 13)**
1 tablespoon fresh mint, chopped
1 teaspoon honey

First cut the top and bottom off the pineapple. Cut around the sides ensuring all the tough skin has been removed. Slice into rounds, remove the central core and then cut into cubes.

Thread a strawberry onto a skewer, then a piece of pineapple, and then an apple cube. Repeat until all skewers are full. Mix together the sugar, cinammon, roasted cumin and chopped mint. Brush the skewers with honey and sprinkle over the spice mixture.

Place on a barbecue or under a hot grill (broiler), turning occasionally, until the sugar has melted and caramelized. Serve hot.

TIP
Apples discolour once they are cut, so plunge them into water with a squeeze of lemon juice.

CLASSICS

It's not easy writing a chapter on classic Indian dishes. From the rich pilaus and marinated meats in the north, to the spicy seafood curries eaten along the coasts, and all in between, India has such a rich and diverse cuisine that I could have written a whole book on classics alone.

The recipes I have included in this chapter are a mix of classic regional dishes that have emerged from India over the last 50 years, but I also wanted to share with you a selection of my own favourites.

For example, I had to include the first dish I ever cooked, Tadka Dal. My recipe has its roots in the western state of Gujarat, but there are a lot of different variations of this lightly spiced yellow lentil soup. And because it's a big Sunday lunch favourite with my family, I thought I must include a recipe for Lamb Shank Rogan Josh, a spiced main meal that originates from Kashmir in the north.

SEAFOOD **caldin**

serves four

200 g (7 oz/2¹/₂ cups) fresh coconut, grated
4 whole black peppercorns
4 whole dried red chillies
2 teaspoons fresh root ginger, sliced
5 cloves garlic
1 teaspoon ground turmeric
1 teaspoon ground coriander
1 teaspoon cumin seeds
1 tablespoon vegetable oil
125 g (4 oz) onions, sliced
125 g (4 oz) scallops
125 g (4 oz) squid rings
200 g (7 oz) mussels
150 g (5 oz) prawns (shrimp), shelled and deveined
1 tablespoon tamarind pulp
2 green chillies, sliced
50 g (2 oz) tomatoes, chopped
75 ml (3 fl oz/¹/₃ cup) coconut milk

A typical coconut-based Goan fish delicacy, spiced with dried red chillies, black peppercorns and tamarind.

In a food processor or blender, grind together the coconut, black peppercorns, dried red chillies, ginger, garlic, ground turmeric, ground coriander and cumin seeds to a smooth paste. Add a little water if necessary.

Heat the oil in a pan and add the onions. Sauté the onions until they are light golden brown. Add the spiced coconut paste. Sprinkle in some water and allow to cook for 15 minutes, adding more water if required.

Add the seafood and mix well. Then add the tamarind pulp and the green chillies and cook for a further 10 minutes.

Add the chopped tomatoes and mix well. Pour in the coconut milk and cook for 5 minutes.

Serve hot with plain basmati rice.

sesame battered TIKKA PRAWNS
Jheenga til tikka

This wonderful dish is a favourite of mine as it has a hint of my favourite spice, mace. Mace is the beautiful red lace that wraps around nutmeg. It is seldom used outside of India and its gives a lovely floral scent when added to dishes.

serves four

1 teaspoon garlic pulp

1 teaspoon ginger pulp

4 tablespoons Patak's Tikka Masala Curry Paste

2 tablespoons plain yoghurt

2 tablespoons grated cheese

1 tablespoon ajowan seeds

2 tablespoons double (heavy) cream

1/2 teaspoon ground mace (optional)

1/2 teaspoon ground green cardamom powder

75 g (3 oz) chickpea (gram) flour

1 kg (2 lbs) large raw prawns (shrimp), cleaned, peeled and deveined with tails left on

25 g (1 oz) sesame seeds

150 g (5 oz) breadcrumbs

vegetable oil for deep-frying

In a bowl mix together all the ingredients except the prawns (shrimp), sesame seeds, breadcrumbs and oil. Add the prawns to the marinade and leave covered in the refrigerator for at least an hour or overnight.

In another bowl combine the sesame seeds and breadcrumbs. Lift each prawn (shrimp) out of the marinade, roll in the sesame seed mix and deep-fry until golden brown, about 10 minutes.

Serve hot with some Fresh coriander (cilantro) and mint dip (see page 15).

TIP

Ajowan seeds and ground mace can be found at all Asian supermarkets.

CRISPY SPICY **fish fillets**

Kurkuri macchi

This dish comes from the southernmost tip of India on the coast, where seafood is plentiful and forms a major part of the diet. It is traditionally made using pomfret, but lemon sole tastes great with the fresh spices.

Serves four

4 fish fillets (a flat fish such as lemon sole is ideal)

5 tablespoons vegetable oil

$1/2$ teaspoon red chilli powder

$1/2$ teaspoon ground turmeric

$1/2$ teaspoon ground coriander

$1/4$ teaspoon ground fennel

1 teaspoon garlic pulp

1 teaspoon ginger pulp

juice of $1/2$ lime

100 g ($3^1/2$ oz/$1/2$ cup) semolina

salt and pepper, to taste

red chilli powder, to season the coating

Pat the fish until it is dry and place on a plate.

In a bowl mix together 1 tablespoon of oil with all the ingredients except the semolina, seasonings and lemon sole. Rub the marinade over the fillets, cover and leave to marinate in the refrigerator for at least two hours.

Sprinkle the semolina on a large plate. Season with salt, pepper and red chilli powder. Remove the fish and place on the semolina. Turn over and crumb the other side. Repeat for the remaining fish fillets.

Heat a shallow frying pan and add the remaining oil. Shallow-fry for 5 minutes before turning over and frying for a further 5 minutes. Allow to drain on absorbent paper. Serve garnished with fresh lime wedges and a Fresh coriander (cilantro) and mint dip (see page 15).

GOAN **fish curry**

This is a mildly spiced creamy dish that comes from the coastal state of Goa. My first memory of tasting it is at a beautiful quaint beachfront restaurant. I have never forgotten the taste.

serves four

flesh of 1 coconut (grated), or 100 g (3^1/2 oz/1^1/4 cups) desiccated coconut

2 teaspoons cumin seeds

3 teaspoons coriander seeds

1 tablespoon fresh root ginger, chopped

4 cloves garlic

1 teaspoon ground turmeric

1 teaspoon black peppercorns

5 tablespoons vegetable oil

150 g (5 oz) onions, sliced

100 ml (3^1/2 fl oz/^{1}/2 cup) coconut milk

600g (1 lb 5 oz) fleshy white fish, such as haddock, cut into 2.5 cm (1 in) cubes

15 g (^{1}/2 oz) tamarind pulp

3 tomatoes, quartered

1 green chilli, sliced

salt, to taste

In a food processor or blender, grind the coconut, cumin seeds, coriander seeds, ginger, garlic, ground turmeric and black peppercorns to a smooth paste, adding a little water if necessary.

Heat the oil in a pan and sauté the onions until golden brown.

Add the ground spice paste and fry for 5 minutes. Add a little water to prevent the paste from burning.

Add the coconut milk and fish and leave to simmer for 10 minutes, stirring occasionally.

Add the tamarind and check the seasoning, adjusting salt if necessary.

Cook for a further two minutes before adding the tomatoes and green chilli and cook for 5 minutes.

Serve hot with basmati rice.

TIP
Goan food is traditionally quite spicy, so if you want to make it more authentic, simply add more green chillies.

SPICY **prawn salad**

Jheenga achaari chaat

Achaari are the spices used to make Indian pickles. One of Patak's first products to hit the shelf was Lime Pickle, which we still sell today. The recipe has remained the same for more than 25 years, and I have been making this salad ever since.

serves four

1¹/2 tablespoons Patak's Lime
  Pickle
¹/2 teaspoon ground turmeric
¹/2 teaspoon black peppercorns,
  crushed
1 teaspoon honey
300 g (11 oz) prawns (shrimp),
  shells removed and deveined
2 tablespoons vegetable oil
¹/4 teaspoon cumin seeds
¹/4 teaspoon fennel seeds
¹/4 teaspoon black mustard
  seeds
1 green chilli, chopped
2.5 cm (1 in) fresh root ginger,
  chopped
100 g (3¹/2 oz) red onions, sliced
1 tablespoon tomato purée
salt, to taste
60 g (2¹/2 oz) green (bell)
  peppers, chopped
60 g (2¹/2 oz) red (bell) peppers,
  chopped
2 tablespoons fresh coriander
  (cilantro), chopped
mixed salad leaves, to serve

In a food processor or blender, purée Patak's Lime Pickle, ground turmeric, crushed black pepper and honey until you have a thick paste. Marinate the prawns (shrimp) in this mixture for at least 1 hour in the refrigerator.

In a pan heat the oil and add the cumin seeds, fennel seeds, mustard seeds, green chilli and ginger. After 2 minutes add the red onions and fry for 10 minutes, until they are golden brown in colour. Add the tomato purée and cook for 10 minutes, sprinkling in some water to prevent the mixture sticking.

Add the prawns (shrimp) and cook for 4 minutes. Check the seasoning and adjust the salt if necessary.

Set the mixture aside to cool slightly before adding the green and red (bell) peppers. Sprinkle over the coriander (cilantro). Serve on a bed of mixed salad leaves.

TIP
If there is any salad left over it is absolutely delicious served on toast the next day.

HOT AND SPICY **courgette prawns**

Kheera jheenga

'Kheera' means courgette (zucchini) and 'Jheenga' means prawns (shrimp). This is a short-cut recipe I developed for my son, Nayan. It originates in Eastern India.

serves four

2 tablespoons vegetable oil

150 g (5 oz/1 cup) onions, sliced

2 tablespoons Patak's Madras Curry Paste

200 g (7 oz) courgettes (zucchini)

450 g (1 lb) large prawns (shrimp), peeled and deveined

salt, to taste

2 tablespoons fresh coriander (cilantro)

In a pan, heat the oil and sauté the onions until translucent, about 5 minutes.

Stir in Patak's Madras Curry Paste and mix well. Cook for 4 minutes. Sprinkle in some water if the mixture begins to stick.

Slice the courgettes (zucchini), add to the pan and stir-fry for a further 8–10 minutes. Add the prawns (shrimp) and cook for 5 minutes. Check the prawns (shrimp) are cooked through, and season to taste, before sprinkling over the coriander (cilantro).

HYDERABADI **fish curry**
Hyderabadi macchi

A delectable recipe from the south-eastern state of Hyderabad which has become world famous in Indian cuisine. The recipe uses a number of dry-roasted spices (see page 13).

serves four

2 teaspoons cumin seeds, dry-roasted
1/2 teaspoon fenugreek seeds, dry-roasted
2 tablespoons desiccated coconut, dry-roasted
2 tablespoons sesame seeds, dry-roasted
3 cloves garlic, crushed
2 teaspoons ground coriander
1/2 teaspoon ground ginger
1/2 teaspoon red chilli powder
1/2 teaspoon ground turmeric
1 teaspoon ground black pepper
4 tablespoons vegetable oil
350 g (12 oz/2 1/2 cups) onions, chopped
450 g (1 lb) cod or haddock fillets, cut into 5 cm (2 in) pieces
1/2 tablespoon tamarind pulp
75 ml (3 fl oz) hot water
salt, to taste

Gently grind together the dry roasted cumin seeds, fenugreek seeds, coconut, sesame seeds and garlic with a pestle and mortar. Stir in the ground coriander, ginger, red chilli powder, turmeric and black pepper.

Heat the oil and add the onions. Cook for 10 minutes before adding the fish. When handling the fish do so gently so it does not break up. Cover the pan and cook for 5 minutes.

Add the spice blend and stir gently.

Mix together the tamarind pulp with the hot water to form a paste. Add this to the fish, cover and leave to simmer for a further 10 minutes. Check the seasoning and serve hot with plain basmati rice.

laced coconut COD

Meen molee

This spicy South Indian fish curry features on many Indian restaurant menus across the globe. I love the crunchy spices.

serves four

2 tablespoons vegetable oil

2 whole dried red chillies

1 teaspoon black mustard seeds

8 fenugreek seeds

8–10 curry leaves, fresh or frozen

4 tablespoons desiccated coconut, soaked in 200 ml (7 fl oz/1 cup) hot water for 20 minutes

2 green chillies, deseeded and cut into quarters lengthways

1 teaspoon ginger pulp

1/2 teaspoon ground turmeric

1 onion, chopped

1/2 teaspoon cumin seeds, roasted and ground (see page 13)

1 teaspoon salt

1/4 teaspoon red chilli powder

1 teaspoon coriander seeds, roasted and ground (see page 13)

1 tablespoon fresh coriander (cilantro), chopped

4 cod or monkfish steaks, about 150–175 g (5–6 oz) each

25 g (1 oz) creamed coconut

juice of 1/2 lemon

basmati rice, to serve

Heat the oil in a shallow pan. Add the dried red chillies, black mustard seeds, fenugreek seeds and curry leaves. When they begin to crackle and the curry leaves turn from green to a light brown, add the coconut (and the water in which it has been soaked). When the liquid starts to boil add the green chillies, ginger, ground turmeric, onion, ground roasted cumin, salt, red chilli powder and ground roasted coriander powder. Add half the coriander (cilantro) leaves and simmer for 3–4 minutes. Immerse the fish into the sauce. Cover and continue cooking for 10 minutes. Add the creamed coconut and cook for a further 2 minutes.

Once the fish has cooked through squeeze in the lemon juice and sprinkle with the remaining coriander. Serve hot with steamed basmati rice.

SLOW-COOKED CHICKEN
with smoked cumin

Jeera murgh

This medium spiced dish originates from North India and combines roasted cumin with fried cumin to give a wonderful flavour.

serves four

3 tablespoons vegetable oil

2 teaspoons cumin seeds

250 g (9 oz/1^1/2 cups) onions, diced

1 green chilli, chopped (optional)

675 g (1^1/2 lbs) chicken thighs, skins removed

4 cloves garlic, chopped

2.5 cm (1 in) piece fresh root ginger, thinly sliced

300 g (11 oz/2 cups) tomatoes, chopped

^{1}/2 teaspoon ground turmeric

In a pan heat the oil and add the cumin seeds. When they begin to crackle add the onions and green chilli and sauté on a medium heat for 5 minutes until they turn translucent.

Add the chicken thighs and allow the meat to seal, this should take about 5 minutes. Add the garlic and ginger and fry for a further 3–4 minutes.

Add the tomatoes, ground turmeric, ground coriander, red chilli powder, salt, garam masala and 2 tablespoons of the fresh coriander (cilantro). Sprinkle in some water. Stir, cover and leave to simmer for about 30 minutes. Add some water if the chicken starts to dry out. The sauce should be thick.

1 teaspoon ground coriander

1 teaspoon red chilli powder

1 teaspoon salt

2 teaspoons ground garam
   masala (see page 14)

3 tablespoons fresh coriander
   (cilantro), chopped

juice of $^1/2$ lemon

1 teaspoon roasted cumin seeds,
   (see page 13), lightly crushed

TIP
Not everyone enjoys eating meat off the
bone so if you prefer, just use boneless
chicken instead.

If it appears too thin leave the pan uncovered and allow the sauce to thicken.

Check that the chicken is cooked through before squeezing over the lemon juice and sprinkling over some roasted cumin seeds and the remaining fresh coriander (cilantro). Cover for 2 minutes to allow the aromas to penetrate, before serving hot with fresh naan.

lamb SHAKUTI

This dish originates from a coastal part of India and tastes great with a simple coconut rice.

serves four

3 tablespoons vegetable oil

125 g (4 oz/$^3/4$ cup) onions,
   sliced

500 g (1 lb 2 oz) lean lamb,
   cubed

4 tablespoons Patak's Madras
   Curry Paste

350 ml (12 fl oz/1$^1/2$ cups) water

125 g (4 oz) chopped tinned
   tomatoes

1 teaspoon garlic pulp

1 teaspoon ginger pulp

1 teaspoon sugar

1 tablespoon fresh coriander
   (cilantro), chopped

salt, to taste

2 tablespoons desiccated coconut

Heat the oil and add the onions. Leave to cook for 10 minutes before adding the lamb. Allow the lamb to seal for a few minutes.

Stir in Patak's Madras Curry Paste. Mix well and pour in the water, tomatoes, garlic, ginger, sugar and half the coriander (cilantro). Adjust the salt, cover and leave to simmer for 45–50 minutes. Stir in the desiccated coconut. Cook for a further 10 minutes. Sprinkle with the remaining coriander (cilantro) and serve with fresh hot Indian bread.

CHICKEN **with** CASHEWS
Balti murgh

The dish originates in the north-west region of India but was perfected by the Mughal invaders. Their cooking techniques have been a wonderful inspiration to the cooking of Northern India and their royal cooks were lavish with their use of nuts.

serves four

2 tablespoons vegetable oil

3 bay leaves

2 tablespoons split coriander seeds

1/2 tablespoon ground mace (optional)

400 g (14 oz/2 cups) onions, finely chopped

250 g (9 oz/1 1/2 cups) tomatoes, chopped

1/2 teaspoon ground turmeric

1 1/2 teaspoons ground cumin

1 1/2 teaspoons ginger pulp

2 cloves garlic

4 tablespoons Patak's Korma Curry Paste

1 kg (2 lb) skinless chicken breast, cut into 2.5–4 cm (1–1 1/2 in) cubes

4 tablespoons cashew nuts, chopped

salt, to taste

4 tablespoons fresh coriander (cilantro), chopped

In a wok or heavy-based frying pan, heat the oil and add the bay leaves, coriander seeds, ground mace (if you are using it) and onions. Cook the onions until translucent and add the tomatoes. Cook for 2–3 minutes. Add the ground turmeric, ground cumin, ginger, garlic and stir in Patak's Korma Curry Paste. Stir and cook for 5 minutes.

Add the chicken, stir, cover and leave the curry to simmer for about 25 minutes. Once the chicken is cooked through, stir in the cashew nuts and cook for a further 5 minutes. Check the seasoning and serve hot garnished with the chopped fresh coriander (cilantro).

73

CLASSICS

LAMB SHANK **Rogan Josh**

A traditional North Indian dish originating in Kashmir. My family and I often eat this when we get together for Sunday lunch.

serves four

4 tablespoons vegetable oil
5 green cardamom pods
2 x 2.5 cm (1 in) pieces of cinnamon stick
3 cloves
2 star anise
2 black cardamom pods (optional)
1/2 teaspoon fennel seeds
1/2 teaspoon cumin seeds
2 dried kashmiri red chillies (dried red chillies will be fine)
500 g (1 lb 2 oz/2 1/2 cups) onions, puréed
1 teaspoon ginger pulp
1 teaspoon garlic pulp
5 tablespoons Patak's Rogan Josh Curry Paste
300 g (11 oz/2 cups) tomatoes, chopped
4 lamb shanks
2 tablespoons fresh coriander (cilantro), chopped

In a large pan heat the oil and add the green cardamom pods, cinnamon sticks, cloves, star anise, black cardamom pods, if using, fennel seeds, cumin seeds and kashmiri red chillies. Allow to sizzle for a few minutes before adding the puréed onions.

Allow the onions to turn golden brown, about 15 minutes, before adding the ginger and garlic.

Add Patak's Rogan Josh Curry Paste and stir well for 2 minutes.

Add the chopped tomatoes and cook for 10 minutes.

Add the lamb shanks. Pour enough water into the pan to cover half of the meat of the lamb shanks. Cover and allow to simmer for about 1½–2 hours, or until the lamb has cooked through. Check occasionally and top up with water when necessary. When the shanks are nearly cooked through, remove from the pan and set aside.

Sprinkle the coriander (cilantro) into the sauce. Remove from the heat and purée the sauce until smooth. Return to the heat and allow to thicken.

Place the lamb shanks back in the sauce for a few minutes to heat through. Serve immediately with hot rice or fresh hot Indian bread.

TIP
Once the shanks have been removed I sometimes skim off the fat that sits on top of the sauce.

LAMB **dhansak**

This dish originates from a special community that settled in India many generations ago. The Parsee community arrived from Persia and the majority lived in my hometown of Mumbai. This is one of my favourites, a mixture of lamb, vegetables and lentils.

serves four

1 tablespoon vegetable oil

2 cloves garlic, sliced

2.5 cm (1 in) fresh root ginger, sliced

2 green chillies, sliced

100 g (3¹/₂ oz/²/₃ cup) onions, chopped

60 g (2¹/₂ oz/¹/₃ cup) yellow lentils (toover dal), soaked in water for an hour

50 g (2 oz/¹/₄ cup) split red lentils (masoor dal), soaked in water for an hour

450 g (1 lb) lamb, cut into 2.5 cm (1 in) cubes

3 tablespoons Patak's Balti Paste

120 g (4 oz/³/₄ cup) tomatoes, chopped

1 tablespoon tomato purée

75 g (3 oz/¹/₂ cup) potatoes, peeled and diced

75 g (3 oz/¹/₂ cup) aubergine (eggplant), diced

100 g (3¹/₂ oz/¹/₂ cup) butternut squash, peeled and diced

250 ml (9 fl oz/1 cup) water

1 tablespoon tamarind pulp

1 tablespoon butter

3 tablespoons fresh mint, chopped

salt, to taste

Heat the oil in a pan and add the garlic, ginger and green chillies. Allow to cook for 2 minutes before adding the onions. Sauté for 5 minutes until light golden brown in colour.

Drain the yellow lentils and red lentils and add to the pan. Cook for 3 minutes and then add the lamb. Cook for about 2–3 minutes.

Stir in the Patak's Balti Paste, chopped tomatoes and tomato purée. Sauté for 2 minutes. Stir well. Add the potatoes, aubergine (eggplant) and butternut squash. Pour in the water. Cover and allow to simmer for 30 minutes or until the lamb is cooked through and the lentils have gone soft.

Add the tamarind, butter and mint and leave to simmer for a further 10 minutes. Check the seasoning and adjust the salt if necessary.

Serve hot with plain basmati rice.

PORK **sorpotel**

This recipe is eaten as an everyday favourite or at special occasions in Northern India. When I make this at home I love to eat it with plain boiled basmati rice and lentils.

serves four

1 teaspoon cumin seeds

6 cloves

2 x 2.5 cm (1 in) pieces of cinnamon stick

¹/4 teaspoon ground nutmeg

3 dried red chillies

10 whole black peppercorns

¹/2 teaspoon ground turmeric

1 teaspoon ground paprika

100 ml (3¹/2 fl oz/¹/2 cup) cider vinegar

1 tablespoon vegetable oil

100 g (4 oz/1 cup) onions, sliced

650 g (1 lb 7 oz) pork tenderloin, cut into 2.5 cm (1 in) strips

4 cloves garlic, chopped

5 cm (2 in) piece fresh root ginger, peeled and finely sliced

3 green chillies, slit lengthways

salt, to taste

chopped spring onions (scallions), to garnish

In a food processor blend together the cumin seeds, cloves, cinnamon sticks, nutmeg, dried red chillies, black peppercorns, ground turmeric, ground paprika and cider vinegar to a fine paste. Set aside.

In a pan heat the oil and gently fry the onions until they turn golden brown, about 10 minutes.

Add the pork and stir-fry for 5 minutes until the meat is sealed.

Add the garlic and ginger and stir-fry for 2 minutes before adding the green chillies and the spice paste. The colour of the sauce will begin to darken after a few minutes. Adjust the salt and check to see whether the pork is cooked through before turning off the heat. Serve garnished with chopped spring onions (scallions).

AUBERGINE AND NEW potato curry

Baingan aloo

Aubergines (eggplants) have always been a comfort food of mine. This is just one of the many recipes that I love to make.

serves four

150 g (5 oz/³/4 cup) new potatoes, cut in half

2 tablespoons vegetable oil

1 teaspoon black mustard seeds

¹/2 teaspoon cumin seeds

1 clove garlic, crushed

2 tablespoons Patak's Madras Curry Paste

200 g (7 oz/1¹/4 cups) tomatoes, chopped

150 g (5 oz/1 cup) aubergines (eggplants), diced

salt, to taste

1 teaspoon sugar

1 tablespoon fresh coriander (cilantro), chopped

1 teaspoon desiccated coconut to garnish

In a pan of boiling water, cook the new potatoes for 15 minutes; until they are almost cooked through yet give some resistance when pierced with a fork. Drain and set aside.

Heat the oil in a pan and add the mustard seeds and the cumin seeds. When they begin to crackle add the garlic and Patak's Madras Curry Paste. Cook for 2 minutes.

Add the chopped tomatoes and bring to the boil.

Add the aubergines (eggplants) and potatoes and cook, covered, at a simmer for 5–10 minutes. Add salt to taste and stir in the sugar.

Serve garnished with fresh coriander (cilantro) and desiccated coconut.

TIP

Aubergines (eggplants) begin to discolour once cut so put them in a bowl of cold water with a squeeze of lemon juice.

POTATO AND YOGHURT **curry**

Dahi wala bateta

This is a curry cooked for afternoon meals in the western state of Gujarat where vegetarian cuisine is a speciality. This is a regular on my menu at home where I serve it with fresh hot chapattis.

serves four

2 tablespoons vegetable oil

2 teaspoons cumin seeds

pinch of fenugreek seeds (optional)

pinch of asafoetida

300 g (11 oz/2 cups) onion, chopped

1 teaspoon ginger pulp

1 teaspoon garlic pulp

600 g (1 lb 5 oz/3 cups) potatoes, peeled, boiled and diced

1¹/2 tablespoons Patak's Madras Curry Paste

6 tablespoons thick natural yoghurt

150 ml (5 fl oz/²/3 cup) water

salt, to taste

fresh coriander (cilantro), to garnish

Heat the oil in a heavy-based pan and add the cumin seeds. When they begin to crackle, add the fenugreek seeds, if using, and asafoetida and then the onions. Sauté until the onions turn translucent.

Add the ginger and garlic and cook for 1–2 minutes before adding the potatoes. Add the Patak's Madras Curry Paste, yoghurt and water. Stir and check the seasoning, adjusting the salt if necessary. Cover partially and let the curry come to the boil. Reduce the heat and simmer for 5–8 minutes. Serve hot garnished generously with coriander (cilantro) leaves.

PAN-FRIED **potato** MASALA
Masala pyaz aloo

Potatoes are popular the world over but nowhere else in the world are there as many exotic preparations as in India. This dish originates in Central India and is traditionally the only accompaniment to hot Indian bread for a hearty breakfast.

serves four

¹/4 teaspoon ground turmeric

450 g (1 lb/2¹/2 cups) potatoes, peeled and thickly sliced

1 tablespoon vegetable oil

¹/4 teaspoon mustard seeds

1 onion, sliced

1 tablespoon Patak's Madras Curry Paste

1 teaspoon lemon juice

salt, to taste

fresh coriander (cilantro) to garnish

Bring a pan of water to the boil and add the ground turmeric. Add the potatoes and boil until just tender. Drain and set aside.

Heat the oil in a frying pan. Add the mustard seeds. When they begin to crackle add the onion. Cook for 5 minutes and add Patak's Madras Curry Paste. Stir well, sprinkling with water to prevent it sticking. Cook for a further 5 minutes before adding the potatoes. Once the potatoes are heated through (this should take about 5 minutes) sprinkle with lemon juice and season to taste. Sprinkle with fresh coriander (cilantro) and serve with hot parathas.

PANEER **tikka**

Paneer is a commonly used ingredient in vegetarian cuisine. It is often described as Indian cottage cheese but this is slightly misleading, as paneer is really a firm cheese that comes in blocks, ready to cut into cubes. This is one of my favourite recipes for paneer.

serves four

- **1 large raw mango, peeled and with the stone removed**
- **50 g (2 oz) fresh coriander (cilantro), chopped**
- **1 tablespoon fresh mint, chopped**
- **3 green chillies, deseeded and chopped**
- **1 tablespoon fresh coconut, grated or desiccated coconut**
- **125 g (4 oz/²/₃ cup) thick natural yoghurt**
- **¹/₄ teaspoon ground green cardamom**
- **pinch of ground cloves**
- **pinch of ground nutmeg**
- **1 tablespoon cream**
- **salt, to taste**
- **400 g (14 oz/2 cups) paneer, cut into 2.5 cm (1 in) cubes**
- **1¹/₂ teaspoons cumin seeds, roasted and ground (see page 13)**
- **1 teaspoon black peppercorns, roasted and ground (see page 13)**

In a blender or food processor, mix together the mango, coriander, mint, green chillies and coconut. Pour into a bowl and mix in the yoghurt, ground green cardamom, ground cloves, ground nutmeg and cream. Check the seasoning and adjust the salt if necessary. Add the paneer and leave to marinate in the refrigerator for 30 minutes.

Remove the paneer from the marinade and thread onto skewers. Cook on a barbecue or in a preheated oven at a moderate heat (200°C/400°F/gas 6) for 10–12 minutes, turning frequently.

In a bowl mix together the ground roasted cumin and ground roasted black pepper.

Generously sprinkle the roasted spice mix over the paneer and serve with Fresh coriander (cilantro) and mint dip (see page 15).

BANARASI **Pilau**

This spiced rice dish originates from the holy city of Banaras in India. It is best served as an accompaniment to a rich curry.

serves four

250 g (9 oz/1¹/4 cups) long grain basmati rice

3 tablespoons vegetable oil

1 teaspoon cumin seeds

3 cloves

3 green cardamom pods

2 bay leaves

150 g (5 oz/1 cup) peas, thawed (if frozen)

150 g (5 oz/³/4 cup) carrots, cut into small cubes

600 ml (1 pint/2¹/2 cups) hot water

Wash the rice in several changes of warm water and leave to soak in cold water for half an hour. Drain in a sieve.

Heat the oil in a heavy pan and add the cumin seeds, cloves, green cardamom pods and bay leaves. After about 2 minutes add the rice and stir gently on medium heat. When all the grains are coated with oil (this usually takes about 3 minutes), add the peas and carrots and pour in the hot water. Add the saffron and salt. Stir and adjust the salt if necessary before leaving to cook uncovered on medium heat for 10 minutes.

When most of the water has been absorbed,

2 strands saffron

3/4 teaspoon salt, to taste

2 tablespoons mixed nuts, such
as pistachios or cashews, sliced

cover, lower the heat and continue cooking for a further 8–10 minutes.

Fluff up the rice with a fork prior to serving. Sprinkle over the sliced nuts and serve piping hot.

TIP
If you prefer, you can pick out the whole spices just before you serve the pilau.

LENTILS with cream and butter
Dal makhni

This is a typical dish originating from Punjab in Northern India. As the title suggests this dish is a high calorie winter warmer. You can replace the butter for oil if you fancy a healthier alternative; personally I love to eat this dish as it is, with fresh hot parathas – delicious.

serves four

3 cloves garlic

1 teaspoon green cardamom pods

2 teaspoons cumin seeds

1 teaspoon cloves

2.5 cm (1 in) piece of cinnamon
stick

50 g (2 oz/1/4 cup) red kidney
beans (rajma), soaked
overnight in water

150 g (5 oz/3/4 cup) black lentils
(urad dal), soaked in water

250 ml (8 fl oz/1 cup) single
(light) cream

3 tablespoons vegetable oil

1/2 teaspoon red chilli powder

salt, to taste

chopped fresh coriander
(cilantro), to garnish

Roughly crush the garlic, green cardamom pods, cumin seeds, cloves and cinnamon using a pestle and mortar. Place this mixture in the centre of a 7.5 cm (3 in) square piece of muslin cloth and tie to form a 'bouquet garni'. Place in a large pan and add the drained kidney beans and black lentils. Add enough water to cover the pulses and bring to the boil. Reduce the heat and leave to simmer for about 1 1/2–2 hours, adding more water if necessary.

Once the mixture has thickened and the pulses are cooked through, remove the 'bouquet garni' and discard. Pour in the cream, butter or oil and add the red chilli powder. Heat through, adjust the salt, and sprinkle in some coriander (cilantro).

PANEER **and** OKRA CURRY
Bhendi paneer

I make this on a regular basis at home. My husband Kirit, loves this vegetarian dish with fresh homemade chapattis.

serves four

250 g (9 oz/1 cup) paneer, cut into 2.5 cm (1 in) cubes
vegetable oil for deep-frying
200 g (7 oz) okra (bhendi), stalky tops removed (see Tip)
2 tablespoons vegetable oil
1 teaspoon cumin seeds
100 g (3^1/$_2$ oz/^{2}/$_3$ cup) onions, chopped
5 cm (2 in) piece of fresh root ginger, chopped
2 green chillies, chopped
140 g (4^1/$_2$ oz/^{3}/$_4$ cup) tomatoes, chopped
^{1}/$_2$ teaspoon red chilli powder
1 teaspoon ground coriander
^{1}/$_2$ teaspoon ground turmeric
250 ml (9 fl oz/1 cup) water
salt, to taste
juice of ^{1}/$_2$ lime
fresh coriander (cilantro) for garnish

Deep-fry the paneer on moderate heat for about 1 minute, or until it turns light golden brown in colour. Drain on absorbent paper. Slice the okra in rounds and deep-fry in the same oil for a few minutes until slightly crispy. Drain on absorbent paper.

Heat the oil in a pan and add the cumin seeds. When they begin to crackle add the onions and sauté for 2 minutes. Add the ginger, green chillies, tomatoes, ground red chilli powder, ground coriander, ground turmeric and cook for 5–6 minutes. Sprinkle in some water if the mixture begins to burn. Add the water and cook for 10 minutes.

Add the paneer to the masala and cook for 2–3 minutes. Then add the okra.

Check the seasoning and adjust the salt. Squeeze in the lime juice.

Sprinkle with fresh coriander (cilantro) and serve hot with fresh Indian bread.

TIP
Okra begins to discolour once cut so deep-fry immediately after slicing.

princess SALAD

Begum ka salaat

Begum is the Urdu word for 'princess' and is often used to describe the lady of the
house. This particular salad is made in North Indian households where there is more
of a Muslim population.

serves four

**100 g (3^1/$_2$ oz) chickpeas,
soaked overnight in water**

**60 g (2^1/$_2$ oz/^{1}/$_2$ cup) green
peas, thawed if frozen**

**300 g (11 oz/1^1/$_2$ cups) potatoes,
peeled and diced**

1 pomegranate (see Tip)

**50 g (2 oz) red (bell) pepper,
chopped**

**50 g (2 oz) green (bell) pepper,
chopped**

**50 g (2 oz/^{1}/$_3$ cup) red onion,
chopped**

**^{1}/$_2$ teaspoon cumin seeds,
roasted and ground (see
page 13)**

^{1}/$_2$ teaspoon red chilli powder

juice of ^{1}/$_2$ lime

sugar, to taste

salt and pepper, to taste

1 tablespoon fresh mint, chopped

Drain the chickpeas and boil in water for
45 minutes until cooked through and soft but not
mushy. Drain and set aside. Blanch the peas in
boiling water for 30 seconds and set aside.

In another pan, boil the potatoes until tender and
allow to cool.

Halve the pomegranate and pick out the seeds
with a fork. Rinse the seeds, drain and place in a
large bowl. Add all the ingredients except the mint
and seasoning. Combine well and season to taste.
Garnish with fresh mint and serve.

TIP
Be careful when preparing pomegranate –
the juice will stain clothes.

raj KORMA

This is one of the first dishes I developed when I joined Patak's. It has always been a favourite of mine.

serves four

3 tablespoons vegetable oil

1 large onion, finely chopped

2 bay leaves

1 clove garlic, diced

4 green cardamom pods, bruised

3 tablespoons fresh coriander (cilantro), chopped

650 g (1 1/2 lb) chicken breast, skin removed and boneless, diced

4 tablespoons Patak's Korma Curry Paste

50 g (2 oz/1/3 cup) tomatoes, chopped

1/2 teaspoon salt

50 ml (2 fl oz/1/4 cup) double (heavy) cream

50 ml (2 fl oz/1/4 cup) natural yoghurt

2 teaspoons desiccated coconut (optional)

Heat the oil in a pan and add the onion and the bay leaves. Cook until the onion begins to turn a light golden brown. Add the garlic, green cardamom pods and half the coriander (cilantro). Add the diced chicken and allow to cook for about 5 minutes, until the meat is sealed.

Add the Patak's Korma Curry Paste and stir. Cover with a lid and leave to cook for 4–5 minutes. Stir in the tomatoes and salt. Continue cooking for another 10–15 minutes or until the chicken is cooked through. Stir in the cream and yoghurt and bring to a simmer. Sprinkle over some desiccated coconut and garnish with the remaining coriander (cilantro) leaves.

PATAK's Traditions

Kirit and Meena on their wedding day in 1976

As with all families we have our traditions that have their roots from way back. Whether from my side or Kirit's they have now become traditions for my children. It is always comforting to know that some of the things you try to pass on to your children do make it through to their adult years. When I was young my mother always taught me the value of working hard and making a career for yourself. Coming from an educated family where both parents had successful jobs, it was easy for me to pass this down to my children. My parents' love of food also found a way into my heart and I too became a foodie from a very young age.

Kirit was not a natural foodie at the beginning. He was pulled out of school to help in the family food business, but his love affair with Indian cuisine soon began, once he learned to appreciate India's rich food heritage. It is no wonder that my three grown up children have all joined the family business and are natural foodies themselves. As a family we love to eat out and we are always chatting about the food we ordered and asking to have a bite of each other's dishes. But there is nothing like a home cooked meal and we have always found these get-togethers to be of the utmost importance. Since my children left home we have always tried to spend Sundays together and it is often a chance for them to come home and have a

much-craved Sunday lunch. One of my favourites which they have been eating since they were young is Raan (slow roast lamb), a recipe passed on from my mother to me. The children love it and I often overhear them telling their friends how much they adore this dish.

Throughout my years of learning and teaching I always emphasised authenticity and good quality food. Indian food has shown many different guises over the last 50 years and I feel it my duty to help people understand the true Indian flavours. It is easy to cook Indian food when you have the right teaching. When I was young we had a cook in my household who was more than happy to pass on his expertise and knowledge of Indian cuisine. He always made sure I understood the regional differences and the wonderful collection of spices and how to cook with them. As with most Indian families the daughters of the family learn how to cook and so following these traditions I have taught my daughter Anjali how to cook. Fortunately my two sons were also enthusiastic and so you could say I had a full class when teaching. Styles change between generations with the introduction of kitchen gadgets and shortcuts whilst cooking, but the fundamental rules have always stayed the same. Of course they have adapted these kitchen skills to suit their lifestyles, but the common factor is great tasting food. They quite happily cook Indian from scratch, but they are also more interested in the shortcuts. The pastes I created 30 years ago are a common ingredient in much of their cooking, but if I am honest, they are in mine too. The versatility and simplicity makes them great to cook with. Whether I am cooking a meal for the family, or a quick snack for myself, they are packed with all the flavours you need to satisfy that spice craving.

As with most girls growing up in India I was taught those fundamental rules about cooking. Rolling a round chapatti and cooking the perfect rice, basmati of course, were high on the agenda. When Anjali was learning to cook she too learnt these two recipes first and then the rest followed. I still remember the day that my grandmother bought me my first rolling pin. I was overjoyed as it meant she was inviting me into her kitchen. She was a lady of secrecy who kept all her recipes to herself – her secret spice blends were never shared. So I felt very privileged to be allowed to work alongside her making the family meals. This tradition is something we have managed to keep within the family as we too have secret spice blends that are known only by my immediate family. Anjali has now started developing her own blends that she is reluctant to share even with me. It is at these times that I remind her whom she learnt her skills from.

Kirit and Meena today

whole green 'tempered' LENTIL DAL

Sabud dal

India is a nation of vegetarians, and lentils are an essential protein in their diet. 'Sabud' means whole and 'dal' is the Indian word for any lentils, whether split or whole. Adding whole fried spices to cooked lentils is a typical North Indian trend.

serves four

175 g (6 oz/1 cup) whole green lentils (masoor dal), soaked in water for an hour

600 ml (1 pint/2^1/$_2$ cups) water

^{1}/$_4$ teaspoon ground turmeric

^{1}/$_4$ teaspoon red chilli powder

^{1}/$_8$ teaspoon fenugreek seeds

^{1}/$_4$ teaspoon fresh root ginger, chopped

^{3}/$_4$ teaspoon salt

1 tomato, chopped

1 tablespoon vegetable oil

1 teaspoon cumin seeds

3 cloves

3 cloves garlic, finely chopped

1 onion, sliced

^{1}/$_4$ teaspoon ground garam masala (see page 14)

1 tablespoon fresh coriander (cilantro), chopped

Drain the lentils. Place the water in a large pan and add the lentils, ground turmeric, red chilli powder, fenugreek seeds, ginger and salt. Bring to the boil, cover and simmer for 40 minutes (during cooking you can add a little extra water if the lentils seem to be getting too dry). Stir in the chopped tomato.

In a frying pan heat the oil and add the cumin seeds and cloves. When they begin to crackle add the garlic and sliced onion. Once the onion begins to brown at the edges turn off the heat.

Bring the lentils to a gentle simmer and pour in the contents of the pan in which you fried the onion (including the oil). Sprinkle with garam masala and fresh coriander (cilantro). Stir and serve hot with fresh Indian bread.

SOUTH INDIAN **lentil curry**

Sambhar

This dish is common in the south of India and is traditionally served with dosas (rice and lentil pancakes) or rice. It makes a great accompaniment.

serves four

5 tablespoons vegetable oil

3 dried red chillies

2 teaspoons coriander seeds

1/2 teaspoon fenugreek seeds

50 g (2 oz/3/4 cup) grated coconut

150 g (5 oz/3/4 cup) yellow lentils (toovar dal)

1/2 teaspoon ground turmeric

75 g (3 oz/2/3 cup) onions, sliced

1/2 teaspoon ground asafoetida

75 g (3 oz/1/2 cup) tomatoes, diced

100 g (4 oz/3/4 cup) aubergine (eggplant), diced

20 g (3/4 oz) tamarind pulp

salt, to taste

1/2 teaspoon sugar

8 curry leaves

1/2 teaspoon black mustard seeds

Heat half the oil in a pan on moderate heat and add the dried red chillies, coriander seeds, fenugreek seeds and grated coconut. Cook, stirring, for 5–10 minutes. Set aside and leave to cool.

Wash the yellow lentils in several changes of water and place in a large pan of water. Bring to the boil, add the ground turmeric and simmer for about 30 minutes. Top up with water if it becomes too dry.

Put the cooled coconut spice mix in a blender or food processor and blitz to a fine paste.

When the lentils become soft and mushy add the sliced onions, asafoetida, diced tomatoes, diced aubergine (eggplant) and coconut paste and continue to cook for 5 minutes. Add the tamarind pulp, salt and sugar and simmer for 2 minutes.

Heat the remaining oil in a separate pan and add the curry leaves and mustard seeds. When they begin to crackle pour them over the lentils. Stir.

Serve hot with plain boiled basmati rice.

TIP

This is a spicy dish, so if you prefer you can reduce the heat by adding fewer dried chillies.

SPICED **puri**

Puris are a puffed bread from Central India. This is a spiced version that I make for my husband Kirit every Saturday morning. We eat them with deep-fried chillies rubbed in salt and asafoetida, simply delicious.

makes 20

225 g (8 oz/2 cups) chapatti atta flour (wholewheat flour), sieved
1/2 teaspoon salt
1/2 teaspoon ground turmeric
pinch of ground asafoetida (optional)
1/4 teaspoon red chilli powder
1 teaspoon ajowan seeds
2 tablespoons chickpea (gram) flour
1 tablespoon vegetable oil
vegetable oil for deep-frying

Combine all the dry ingredients in a bowl and mix thoroughly. Add the 1 tablespoon of vegetable oil and rub into the flour. Add some warm water (a little at a time) and knead the flour to form a soft dough. Cover with a damp cloth and let the dough rest for 20–25 minutes.

Knead again and divide into 20 equal portions. Shape into round balls and then flatten into round discs 7.5 cm (3 in) in diameter using a rolling pin.

Heat the oil in a large heavy-based pan until the temperature reaches 190°C (375°F). Reduce the heat to low and fry the puris one at a time, easing them into the oil with a slotted spoon. When they puff up (almost immediately), turn over and cook on the other side. Each puri should take about 1 minute to fry and puff up half way through cooking.

Remove the puri with a slotted spoon and drain on kitchen paper. They are best eaten hot.

TIP

When rolling out the puris, smear a little oil on the surface. I find this stops the puris sticking to the rolling pin.

SPICED **vegetable medley**
Tamatar gobi sem masaledar

This is a great vegetarian dish made using mustard and garlic. You can use any vegetables you like but I think the combination of French beans and cherry tomatoes works wonderfully together.

serves four

225 g (8 oz/1 cup) cauliflower, cut into florets

225 g (8 oz) French beans or fine green beans

8 cherry tomatoes

2 tablespoons vegetable oil

2 teaspoons black mustard seeds

3 cloves garlic, chopped

1/4 teaspoon red chilli powder

1 teaspoon sugar

1/4 teaspoon ground turmeric

1/4 teaspoon fresh root ginger, grated

1 green chilli, chopped (optional)

salt, to taste

1/4 teaspoon ground garam masala (see page 14)

Wash the cauliflower and trim the beans into 2.5–4 cm (1–1 1/2 in) lengths. Cut the tomatoes into halves.

Heat the oil in pan and add the mustard seeds. Once they begin to crackle add the garlic and fry until a light golden colour.

Add the cauliflower and beans, sprinkle in some water and sauté for 5 minutes or until the florets begin to colour.

Add the red chilli powder, sugar, ground turmeric, ginger, green chilli, if using, and check the salt. Cover and cook on medium heat for about 15 minutes. Sprinkle in some water if the mixture begins to stick.

Turn off the heat. Toss the tomatoes in the mixture and sprinkle with garam masala.

Serve hot with some fresh parathas.

tomato CHUTNEY

Different variations of this classic chutney can be found all over India and will vary from region to region. I love this version which originates from South India. I eat it with almost anything.

serves four

1 tablespoon vegetable oil

1 teaspoon black mustard seeds

10 curry leaves

2 teaspoons fresh root ginger, chopped

1 green chilli, chopped

1 kg (2 lb 4 oz/7 cups) tomatoes, chopped

2 teaspoons ground coriander

1/2 teaspoon ground turmeric

1 teaspoon ground cumin

salt, to taste

1 tablespoon sugar

1 tablespoon vinegar

In a pan heat the oil and add the mustard seeds, curry leaves, ginger and green chilli. After 2 minutes add the tomatoes. Cook for about 5 minutes before adding the ground coriander, ground turmeric and ground cumin. Cook for 5 minutes and add the salt, sugar and vinegar.

Continue cooking for 10 more minutes before removing from the heat. Leave to cool before chilling in the refrigerator. This is a wonderful dip to serve with poppadums.

TADKA DAL

This is one of my favourite recipes, which I have eaten since I was a young girl. It goes on my list of comfort foods. Yellow lentils are known as toover dal.

serves four

250 g (9 oz/1¹/4 cups) yellow lentils

1 litre (1¹/2 pints/3 cups) water

1 teaspoon ground turmeric

3 tablespoons vegetable oil

1 teaspoon black mustard seeds

1 teaspoon cumin seeds

1 green chilli, chopped

1 teaspoon ginger pulp

¹/2 teaspoon red chilli powder

¹/2 teaspoon asafoetida

225 g (8 oz) tomatoes, chopped

juice of ¹/2 lemon

salt, to taste

chopped fresh coriander
  (cilantro), to garnish

Wash the lentils in several changes of water and place in a large pan with the water. Add the ground turmeric and cook on moderate heat for about 45 minutes.

In a small pan heat the oil and add the mustard seeds and cumin seeds. When they begin to crackle add the green chilli and ginger. After 1 minute add the red chilli powder and asafoetida. Cook for a further minute before adding the chopped tomatoes. Stir well and allow to cook for a few minutes.

Check the lentils are cooked through – they will have split and gone mushy. Pour in all the spiced tomato mixture (tadka) including the oil. Squeeze in the lemon juice and season with salt. Sprinkle in some coriander (cilantro) and serve piping hot with plain boiled basmati rice.

SPECIAL
OCCASIONS

I always try to get back to India to celebrate Diwali, the
biggest and most famous annual Hindu festival. Also known as 'The
Festival of Lights', it's a chance for families to come together, so the
feasts are worth the trip alone. One thing I love about Diwali is
seeing the street sellers making fresh jalebis, because it reminds me
of where Patak's began. I have included some traditional Indian
dishes, some with a twist, such as my Creamy vanilla rice pudding.
It is often eaten at weddings but you don't need an excuse or a
special occasion to enjoy these recipes; they're great anytime.

THE EMPEROR'S **biryani**
Badshai biryani

This is the masterpiece of many Northern Indian cooks and is often the central dish at festive dinners. It is quite a laborious dish, so I have simplified it to make it easier.

serves four

250 g (9 oz/1¹/4 cups) basmati rice

4 tablespoons vegetable oil

300 g (11 oz/2¹/3 cups) onions, sliced

150 g (5 oz/1 cup) onions, finely chopped

675 g (1¹/2 lbs) lean lamb, diced in 2.5 cm (1 in) cubes

4 tablespoons Patak's Tikka Masala Curry Paste

2 tomatoes, chopped

1 tablespoon natural yoghurt

5 green cardamom pods

2.5 cm (1 in) piece of cinnamon stick

2 bay leaves

a few saffron strands

salt, to taste

3 tablespoons fresh coriander (cilantro), chopped

TIP

If you prefer, you can remove the whole spices after the rice is cooked.

Wash the rice in several changes of warm water. Soak in cold water for 20–25 minutes.

Heat 3 tablespoons of oil and fry the sliced onions until golden brown. Remove from the pan and place on absorbent paper.

In the same oil, sauté the chopped onions for 5 minutes. Once they are light golden brown add the lamb and allow to seal for about 3 minutes. Brown the meat before adding the Patak's Tikka Masala Curry Paste. Pour in about 150 ml (5 fl oz) of water to prevent the meat from burning. Add the chopped tomatoes and yoghurt and cook for 5 minutes before covering and leaving to cook on a medium heat for about 30 minutes.

Meanwhile, drain the soaked rice. In a pan heat the remaining tablespoon of oil. Sauté the rice for 1 minute and then add the green cardamom pods, cinnamon stick, bay leaves, saffron strands and salt (about 1 teaspoon). Add enough boiling water to cover the rice. Cook over a medium high heat for 12–15 minutes, or until the rice is cooked. Drain and then divide the rice into 3 equal portions.

Check the lamb is cooked and the sauce has thickened before dividing into 2 equal portions.

Grease an ovenproof dish (such as a casserole dish) and layer the bottom first with aromatic rice, then sprinkle with chopped coriander (cilantro), and then spread a layer of lamb followed by another sprinkling of chopped coriander (cilantro). Repeat the layering until all rice and lamb has been used. Seal the dish tightly and cook in a preheated oven at a moderate heat (190°C/375°F/gas 5) for 10 minutes.

Garnish with the sliced fried onions and fresh coriander (cilantro).

WILTED SPINACH **and tomato rice**
Palak tamatar chawal

This unique combination originates in the Central Plains of India. This is one I make for guests at dinner parties.

serves four

250 g (9 oz/1 1/4 cups) basmati rice
2 tablespoons vegetable oil
3/4 teaspoon cumin seeds
2.5 cm (1 in) piece of cinnamon stick
6 cloves
6 green cardamom pods
3 bay leaves
125 g (4 oz/1 cup) onions, sliced
1/2 teaspoon black pepper, roughly crushed
1 clove garlic, crushed
1/2 teaspoon fresh root ginger, grated
1/2 teaspoon ground garam masala (see page 14)
1 teaspoon ground coriander
1 teaspoon ground cumin
1/4 teaspoon ground turmeric
3/4 teaspoon salt
150 g (5 oz/1 cup) fresh tomatoes, chopped
75 g (3 oz) spinach leaves
2 tablespoons fresh coriander (cilantro), chopped

Wash the rice in several changes of water and then leave to soak in cold water for 20 minutes before draining well.

Heat the oil in a pan and add the cumin seeds together with the cinnamon stick, cloves, green cardamom pods and bay leaves. When the seeds begin to crackle add the sliced onion. Sauté until golden brown then add the drained rice. Lower the heat and gently fry the rice, tossing and folding continually. Ensure that the rice does not begin to stick to the pan. After 4–5 minutes each grain of rice will be coated with the oil.

Add the black pepper, garlic, ginger, garam masala, ground coriander, ground cumin, ground turmeric, salt and tomatoes. Stir and cook for 3–4 minutes before adding enough boiling water to a level 1 cm (½ in) above the layer of rice. Allow to cook over a medium heat. When the water begins to boil, cover the pan. Reduce the heat and simmer for 8–10 minutes until all the water has been absorbed and the rice is cooked.

Sprinkle over the spinach leaves and fold through the rice. Fluff up the rice, and serve garnished with chopped coriander (cilantro).

Serve hot as an accompaniment to a main dish.

LIGHT TOMATO SOUP **with baby spinach**

Palaki rasam

This recipe is close to my heart as it reminds me of wintertime as a child. Its roots are from coastal parts of South India. I now make this at special occasions when my family gets together.

serves four

75 g (3 oz/^{1}/2 cup) yellow lentils (toover dal), soaked in water for at least 1 hour

2 tablespoons vegetable oil

2–3 star anise

2–3 bay leaves

5 cm (2 in) piece of fresh root ginger, chopped

600 g (1 lb 5 oz/4^1/2 cups) tomatoes, chopped

1 green chilli, chopped

^{1}/4 teaspoon red chilli powder

^{1}/2 teaspoon ground coriander

2 tablespoons fresh coriander (cilantro), chopped

600 ml (1 pint/2^1/2 cups) water

50 g (2 oz/^{1}/4 cup) carrots, cut into cubes

50 g (2 oz/^{1}/4 cup) potatoes, diced

salt and pepper, to taste

juice of ^{1}/2 lime

100 g (3^1/2 oz) baby spinach, washed

Drain the lentils.

Heat the oil in a pan and add the star anise and bay leaves. Once they begin to crackle add the drained lentils, ginger, tomatoes, green chilli, red chilli powder, ground coriander and water. Allow to simmer for 45 minutes. Stir the broth occasionally to prevent it sticking, and top up with water if necessary.

Remove the star anise and bay leaves and pour the broth into a food processor or blender and blend until smooth. Pass through a sieve and place back on the heat. Add the carrots, potatoes and fresh coriander (cilantro) and season with salt and pepper. Squeeze in the lime juice. Cook for about 10 minutes, or until the vegetables are tender. Add the baby spinach and check the seasoning.

Cook for a further two minutes. Serve hot with fresh naan.

ONION AND CORIANDER **paratha**
Pyazi dhania paratha

There are over 80 varieties of breads in India – some leavened and the majority unleavened. They are made with wholewheat flour or 'atta', sometimes cooked on griddles or deep-fried in 'kadhais'. Normal, everyday breads are not flavoured because they are eaten with spicy curries. However, this particular one is more of a snacking bread.

Makes four to six parathas

250 g (9 oz/2 cups) chapatti atta flour (wholewheat flour)
100 g (3¹/2 oz/³/4 cup) red onion, sliced
¹/2 teaspoon fresh root ginger, grated
¹/2 teaspoon red chilli powder
1 teaspoon salt
1 tablespoon fresh coriander (cilantro)
pinch of asafoetida (optional)
3 teaspoons vegetable oil
125 ml (4 fl oz/¹/2 cup) warm water
3 tablespoons flour for rolling and dusting
6 tablespoons oil to brush when frying

TIP
I love to eat these dipped into fresh hot Chai (see page 17).

In a bowl combine the flour with the red onion, ginger, red chilli powder, salt, coriander (cilantro) and asafoetida (if using). Mix well. Rub in 3 teaspoons of vegetable oil. Gradually add the water, a little at a time, mixing everything together to make a pastry-like dough (it should be soft). Do not add all the water at once as if too much water is added the dough will be very sticky and difficult to roll.

Divide into 4–6 equal balls (depending on the size you want).

Heat a cast iron frying pan until very hot. Flatten each ball and dust with flour. Using a rolling pin, roll each ball into a 15 cm (6 in) disc on a rolling board or flat surface.

Transfer to the hot pan and let it cook for 1 minute before turning it over. Brush the cooked side with oil and turn over again. Brush the second side with oil and turn over again for 20 seconds.

Remove and put on a plate whilst you make the other parathas.

These can be served cold but they are best hot.

DIWALI

Diwali, also known as 'The Festival of Lights', marks the beginning of the lunar New Year for Indians. Celebrated by Hindus, Sikhs and Jains, it falls at some point within October and November with the exact date depending on the lunar calendar. For Hindus, the five-day festival symbolises an escape from darkness and allows them to focus on the true and positive values of life.

The word 'Diwali' originates from 'Deepavali' with 'Deepa' meaning 'light', and 'Avali' meaning 'a row'. This comes from tiny lamps being lit and placed outside homes to welcome the goddess of wealth and prosperity, Lakshmi. The Hindu god Vishnu also has particular significance during Diwali. As Prince Rama, one of his many incarnations, he was exiled by a wicked stepmother who wanted her own son to be king. When, after 14 years, Rama returned, his path was lit with burning lamps welcoming him home. In India, the lamps are traditionally fuelled by mustard oil and floated across the River Ganges. It's considered a good omen if the lamps reach the other side. Rangolis, traditional motifs made out of brightly coloured powders, also appear outside homes, often in the shape of the auspicious lotus leaf held by the goddess Lakshmi.

Fireworks play a big part in Diwali celebrations

In the days leading up to Diwali, houses are renovated and given a fresh coat of brightly coloured paint. During the festival, Indians all over the world get together to dance, light fireworks and exchange gifts and ornately decorated boxes of exotic nuts and dried fruits. And with Diwali also marking the beginning of the financial year, business owners visit their local temple to be blessed for a successful year ahead.

I love travelling back to India during this time. The streets are always bustling, the local shrine is always filled with men and women dressed up in their favourite saris and finest jewellery to worship all the religious gods and

Saffron, the most prized spice, is used extensively in cooking during Diwali

there's a really happy atmosphere everywhere you go. It's the Hindu equivalent of New Year and is the perfect excuse to celebrate.

As for food, there's an astonishing array on offer and it's not uncommon for over 100 desserts to be offered to the gods for blessing. The specialities vary from state to state, but food is always the highlight of the celebrations. Sweet puddings are made using expensive aromatic spices such as cardamom and saffron, and favourite dishes include 'Banarasi Pilau' and 'Jalebis'.

Diwali is increasingly celebrated in countries all over the world, not just in India. With such a wonderful choice of dishes on offer, why not try cooking your own Diwali meal. So join in the fun of Diwali and experiment with Indian spices and ingredients to cook up some authentic Indian feasts.

SLOW ROAST **lamb**
Raan

This recipe is often found in the romantic Kashmir Valley at the foothills of the Himalayas, in the North of India. The dish is often served at festive occasions, as it is very impressive.

serves four

150 g (5 oz/1 cup) onions, sliced
1.8 kg (4 lbs) lean leg of lamb
250 g (9 oz/1²/₃ cups) onions, chopped
6 cloves garlic, chopped
2.5 cm (1 in) fresh root ginger, grated
25 g (1 oz) almonds, blanched
2 green chillies, chopped
250 ml (9 fl oz) natural yoghurt
3 tablespoons ground coriander
2 tablespoons ground cumin
¹/₂ teaspoon ground garam masala (see page 14)
¹/₄ teaspoon salt
4 tablespoons vegetable oil
6 cloves
2.5 cm (1 in) piece of cinnamon stick
8 black peppercorns
10 green cardamom pods
1 tablespoon almond slivers, to garnish

Place the sliced onions in the bottom of a roasting dish and place the lamb on top. Make deep gashes all over the lamb. This will allow the spices to penetrate through the lamb.

In a food processor or blender combine the chopped onions, garlic, ginger, blanched almonds, green chillies and 3 tablespoons of yoghurt until they form a coarse mixture.

In a bowl combine the remainder of the yoghurt with the ground coriander, ground cumin, garam masala and salt. Add the blended paste to the onion mixture and stir.

Fill the gashes in the lamb with the paste and smear a little over the lamb. Cover and leave to marinate for 8 hours or so in the refrigerator. Remove and bring back to room temperature.

In a frying pan heat the oil and add the cloves, cinnamon stick, peppercorns and cardamom pods. When the cloves and cardamom pods begin to swell, turn off the heat and sprinkle the spices and the oil onto the lamb.

Bake in a preheated oven, at a high heat (220°C/425°F/gas 7) for 12–15 minutes so the meat begins to take on some colour. Cover with foil, and lower the heat to 170°C/330°F/gas 3½ and bake for a further 2 hours.

Before serving, baste with the juices from the dish.

Serve garnished with almond slivers and a simple cumin-infused rice.

SMOKED AUBERGINES **with chives**
Baingan bhartha

Aubergines (eggplants) are a popular vegetable throughout the subcontinent of India. This particular dish was originally cooked on charcoal fires and had a unique smoky flavour. Most homes, however, have adapted this recipe to be cooked in the oven, or if one has the patience, on a gas flame. It is a wonderful accompaniment to an Indian meal.

This is my husband Kirit's favourite dish. In my early years of marriage I used to have to cook this for him and his extended family. Now I cook it for mine.

serves four

2 large aubergines (eggplants)

little oil for rubbing on the aubergines (eggplants)

2 tablespoons vegetable oil

¹/2 teaspoon black mustard seeds

1 teaspoon cumin seeds

3 spring onions, chopped

2 tablespoons chives, chopped

1 green chilli, chopped

2 tomatoes, chopped

¹/4 teaspoon ground turmeric

¹/4 teaspoon red chilli powder

1 teaspoon ground coriander

1 teaspoon ground cumin

³/4 teaspoon salt

¹/8 teaspoon ground garam masala (see page 14)

1 tablespoon fresh coriander (cilantro), chopped

3 tablespoons plain yoghurt

Prick the aubergines (eggplants) a few times with a fork and rub each one with oil. Wrap in foil and bake in a preheated oven, moderate heat (200°C/400°F/gas 6) for 40 minutes. At the end of the 40 minutes the aubergines should be 'pulpy'.

Take out of the foil and spoon the juices and pulp into a bowl and mash with a fork, discarding the skins.

Heat the oil in a pan and add the mustard seeds and cumin seeds. When they begin to crackle add the spring onions, chives and green chilli and fry for 5–7 minutes on medium heat. Add the tomatoes, ground turmeric, red chilli powder, ground coriander, ground cumin and salt and cook for a further 2–3 minutes. Add the mashed aubergine (eggplant). Fold in the spices, stir, cover and cook for 10–12 minutes.

Sprinkle with garam masala and fresh coriander (cilantro) and drizzle with yoghurt. Serve as an accompaniment to main dishes, or as a snack with hot chapattis.

Smoked aubergines (eggplants) with chives

CREAMY VANILLA rice pudding

Kheer

This is a favourite dish served at Indian weddings. I now always associate it with happy occasions.

serves four

1.5 litres (2¹/2 pints/6 cups) milk

175 g (6 oz/³/4 cup) basmati rice or pudding rice

¹/2 bay leaf

1 vanilla pod

125 g (4 oz/¹/2 cup) sugar

125 g (4 oz/³/4 cup) raisins

¹/4 teaspoon ground green cardamom

In a large saucepan combine the milk, rice and bay leaf. Slit the vanilla pod down the centre lengthways, and with the back of the knife remove the seeds. Place these in the pan with the vanilla pod.

Cook on a high heat for 15 minutes, stirring very frequently. Bring to a boil and then lower the heat. Simmer for about 40 minutes or until it thickens. Remove the bay leaf and the vanilla pod and add the sugar, raisins and ground green cardamom. Remove from the heat and allow to cool. It will thicken as it cools. Refrigerate until cold.

TIP

Kheer can be served warmed but I prefer mine straight from the refrigerator.

INDIA'S **favourite dessert**
Jalebis

This is known as the nation's favourite dessert – and one of the most difficult to make! Everyone loves the sweet stickiness, especially my late father-in-law. L.G. Pathak (the founder of Patak's) and his wife started making this dessert in their tiny shop in London. From those humble beginnings, Patak's is now a household name. This dish holds a special place in all my family's hearts.

**500 g (1 lb 2 oz/6 cups) plain
  (all-purpose) white flour**
¹/₄ teaspoon saffron
6 green cardamom pods
750 g (1 lb 11 oz/4¹/₂ cups) sugar
juice of ¹/₂ lime
ghee for frying
flaked almonds, to decorate

Sieve the flour into a stainless steel bowl. Add water to the flour, a little at a time, until you get a thick creamy consistency. Cover the bowl and leave to ferment in a warm place for 24 hours. At the end of this time the mixture will have doubled in size and tiny bubbles will have formed on the surface.

In a metal bowl, gently heat the saffron on a low heat, shaking occasionally so that the threads of

saffron do not stick to the hot bowl. After a few minutes you will be able to smell the sweet aroma. Remove from the heat and set aside. Once cool, crush it with your fingers. Peel the green cardamom pods and pound the seeds with a pestle and mortar until coarse.

In the same metal bowl used for the saffron, add 600 ml (1 pint) water. Add the sugar and place on a moderate heat. Allow it to boil until it starts to thicken. Squeeze in the lime juice. Remove the froth that gathers on the surface of the sugar syrup so that the liquid is crystal-clear. Add the crushed saffron. When the syrup thickens it will leave a line when drizzled, add the pounded cardamom seeds and husks. Bring to the boil and then remove from the heat.

Heat a heavy-based wide pan and add the ghee. Once heated, lower the flame.

Remove the cover from the batter, beat for a few minutes. Make a small hole in the centre of a thick square cloth. Fill with some batter. Gather the four ends of the cloth to make it into a bag-type bundle. Hold the bag over the heated ghee and gently begin pressing the bundle, moving it in a circular motion. Make the outer circle about 7.5 cm (3 in) in diameter, and then continue to create inner circles. Then move on to another circle, repeating the same motion. Once you have made 4 or 5 jalebis leave them to cook. They will turn light golden brown after a few minutes. Turn over and repeat on the other side until the jalebis are crispy.

Lift them out using a slotted spoon or metal skewer, and allow all the excess ghee to drain off back into the pan. Place them directly in the sugar syrup and leave to soak for 5 minutes. Remove from the syrup and serve hot, decorated with flaked almonds.

PUDDINGS
AND

DESSERTS

No cookery book would be complete without a chapter on desserts, and Indians are well known for their love of sweet things. Most of my recipes are classics with an Indian touch. Whether it's Cinnamon crème brûlée, or Iced cardamom coffee, each is a suitably sweet way to end any Indian meal.

molten CHOCOLATE PUDDING

My eldest son Neeraj adores this dessert. The title speaks for itself.

serves four

butter for moulds

flour for dusting moulds

100 g (3^1/$_2$ oz) unsalted butter

100 g (3^1/$_2$ oz) dark chocolate (70% cocoa)

2 eggs

2 egg yolks

50 g (2 oz/^{1}/$_3$ cup) caster sugar

60 g (2^1/$_2$ oz/^{3}/$_4$ cup) plain (all-purpose) flour

1 teaspoon cocoa powder

Butter the insides of 4 ramekin dishes or individual pudding moulds. Dust with flour and then empty out the excess flour.

Place the butter and broken up chocolate in a heatproof bowl. Place over a saucepan of simmering water and allow the chocolate to melt slowly. Stir and leave to cool.

Place the eggs and the egg yolks in a bowl and add the sugar. Whisk the mixture until pale, thick and it has doubled in volume. The mixture should leave a trail when spooned.

Fold in the melted chocolate mixture. Sift in the flour and fold in with a large metal spoon. Divide the pudding mixture equally between the four moulds ensuring there is enough space at the top of the moulds for it to rise slightly.

Cook in a preheated oven at 180°C/350°F/gas 4 for 15–18 minutes. They should wobble slightly but still be set. Allow to rest for 1 minute before placing a shallow bowl on top, tipping upside down and easing the pudding out, being careful not to let it break. Dust with a little cocoa powder and serve with pouring cream or custard.

mango CARPACCIO

This simple healthy dessert is quick to make and is a refreshing finish to any meal.

serves four

2 large ripe mangoes, peeled
50 g (2 oz/1/4 cup) demerara
  sugar
2 tablespoons water
5 fresh mint leaves
juice of 1/2 lime
pinch of dried red chilli flakes
  (optional)
3 green cardamom pods, lightly
  crushed

Slice the mango into wafer thin slices and lay on a large plate.

In a pan heat the sugar with the water on a low flame until all the sugar has dissolved and the liquid has become a syrup. This should take about 5 minutes. Bring the syrup to the boil and add the mint leaves, lime juice, chilli flakes (if using) and green cardamom pods. Allow the flavours to release in the syrup for a few minutes before removing from the heat.

Leave the syrup to cool slightly before drizzling over the mango.

CLASSIC LASSI

The best way to calm the heat of a spicy dish is to drink an ice-cold lassi. Yoghurt has many health-giving properties and this drink is perfect for settling the stomach. It can be served sweet or salty.

serves four

400 g (14 oz/3 1/4 cups) natural
  yoghurt
75 g (3 oz/1/2 cup) sugar or
  1 1/2 teaspoons salt
1 teaspoon roasted cumin seeds,
  crushed (see page 13)
pistachio slivers, to garnish

Pour the yoghurt into a bowl, add the sugar or salt and 200 ml (7 fl oz) chilled water. Whisk well until all the lumps of yoghurt have broken down and all the sugar or salt has dissolved. The lassi should be smooth. Stir in the roasted cumin seeds. Garnish with pistachio. Drop in some crushed ice to keep the lassi cool before serving.

TIP

For a delicious mango lassi just add the flesh of 2 ripe mangoes with the water and yoghurt. Add sugar to taste and blend in a food processor until smooth.

cinnamon CRÈME BRÛLÉE

Whenever I eat out at a restaurant I always choose crème brûlée from the dessert menu. This is my recipe with a hint of cinnamon for a different twist.

serves four

175 ml (6 fl oz/3/4 cup) milk

175 ml (6 fl oz/3/4 cup) cream

1 teaspoon ground cinnamon,
  plus extra for dusting

1 vanilla pod

2 eggs

3 1/2 tablespoons honey

pinch of salt

brown sugar, for topping

ground cinnamon, for dusting

TIP

It is sometimes tricky pouring boiling water into the roasting tray and then carrying it over to the oven, so I just place them in the oven and then pour in the water.
If you can't get hold of vanilla pods, use vanilla extract.

Slit the vanilla pod down the centre lengthways and remove the seeds. Place both pod and seeds in a pan with the milk, cream, ground cinnamon and heat gently until warm.

In a large bowl whisk together the eggs, honey and salt. Slowly pour in the milk mixture making sure you whisk continuously until all the milk has been added and the mixture is fully blended. Strain and divide into four ramekins.

Place them in a roasting tray. Pour boiling water into the roasting tray so that it comes halfway up the sides of the ramekins. Bake in a preheated oven at a low heat (150°C/300°F/gas 2) for 45 minutes.

Remove from the oven and allow to cool before placing in the refrigerator overnight.

When you are ready to serve sprinkle the tops of the chilled cinnamon custards with brown sugar and place under a very hot grill for about 1 minute, until the sugar has melted and turned deep golden brown. Sprinkle with a light dusting of ground cinnamon before serving.

MANGO **and** CHILLI SORBET

Sorbets are often served in between dishes to clean the palate so you are ready to taste the flavours of the next dish. This can be eaten in between or as a dish on its own.

serves four

1 large mango, peeled and sliced

40 g (1 1/2 oz/1/4 cup) caster
  sugar

juice of 1/2 lime

1 teaspoon dried red chilli flakes

75 ml (3 fl oz/1/3 cup) water

fresh lime zest, to garnish

finely sliced red chilli, to garnish

In a food processor or blender mix together the mango, sugar, lime juice, chilli flakes and water to form a purée. Tip into a plastic freezer-proof tub and seal well. Place in the freezer for 2–3 hours, removing every 30 minutes to stir.

Once the sorbet is almost set remove from the freezer and scoop into serving dishes. Garnish with the fresh lime zest and strips of red chilli.

PINEAPPLE **pudhina**

I love eating fruit for dessert and I am always thinking of new and exciting ways to add a little flavour to even the simplest dishes. This is one of my favourites.

serves four

1 whole pineapple
2 tablespoons sugar
7 fresh mint leaves
juice of ¹/2 lime

TIP
I often serve this dessert with a spoon of crème fraîche.

Cut the top and bottom off the pineapple and cut around the sides ensuring all the tough skin has been removed. Slice into rounds and then remove the central core. Cut the hollow rounds into cubes.

Use a pestle and mortar to mix together the sugar, mint leaves and lime juice. Once combined sprinkle over the pineapple and allow to rest for 5 minutes before serving.

ICED CARDAMOM **coffee**

This is a great after-dinner drink. The cardamom and the coffee are a wonderful combination.

serves four

4 cups of freshly made coffee
1 teaspoon ground green cardamom
4 teaspoons sugar
2.5 cm (1 in) piece of cinnamon stick
1 teaspoon ground almonds
4 tablespoons double (heavy) cream
4 green cardamom pods, to garnish
flaked almonds, to garnish

Brew 4 cups of coffee using your favourite brewing method. If you are grinding the beans yourself then add the ground green cardamom before grinding. If not then add the ground green cardamom after you have brewed the coffee. Add the sugar, cinnamon stick and ground almonds and mix into the hot coffee. Allow the sugar to dissolve before leaving the coffee to cool.

When ready to serve, half fill the serving glasses with crushed ice. Strain the coffee and pour into the glasses. Rest the back of a spoon on top of the coffee and gently run 1 tablespoon of cream over the back of the spoon. It will rest on top in a thick layer. Serve garnished with a green cardamom pod and flaked almonds.

SAFFRON **semolina pudding**
Rava kesari

Saffron is the world's most expensive spice. It is used when making dishes for special occasions. This particular recipe is made during Diwali (Hindu Festival of Lights) but once you taste it, you will want to make it more than just once a year.

serves four

1 1/2 teaspoons ghee (clarified butter)
15 cashew nuts, roughly chopped
15 raisins
3 green cardamom pods, lightly crushed
150 g (5 oz/3/4 cup) semolina
75 g (3 oz/1/2 cup) sugar
300 ml (1/2 pint/1 cup) milk
pinch of saffron strands
slivers of pistachio, to garnish (optional)

Heat the ghee in a pan and add the cashew nuts and raisins and green cardamom pods. Cook for about 2 minutes before adding the semolina. Reduce the heat and cook, stirring continuously, for 2 minutes.

Mix in the sugar and pour in the milk. Add the saffron strands and cook over a low to medium heat, whisking well.

When the mixture begins to thicken and the semolina is cooked remove from the heat. Garnish with the pistachios and serve hot.

SUMMER **cooler**
Jal jeera

This drink can be described as a cumin-flavoured appetiser.

serves four

750 ml (1 1/2 pints/4 cups) water
1 tablespoon tamarind pulp
10 fresh mint leaves
1 teaspoon ground cumin
2 teaspoons dark brown sugar
1 1/2 teaspoons sea salt
1 teaspoon ground black pepper
1 teaspoon ginger pulp
juice of 1/2 lime
few extra mint leaves for garnish

Pour the water into a jug and stir in the tamarind pulp. Mix well.

Grind up the mint leaves in a pestle and mortar and add to the water. Stir in the cumin, sugar, salt and pepper. Stir until the sugar and salt dissolve and add the ginger and lime juice.

Leave to chill for a few hours in the refrigerator and then strain. Pour over ice cubes and garnish with a few mint leaves.

SUMMER FRUITS **crunchy crumble**

This is different from an ordinary fruit crumble as it has lovely aromatic spices adding a little something to the dish. I have chosen summer fruits for this recipe, but you can use any fruits you fancy.

serves four

200 g (7 oz) raspberries

150 g (5 oz) blackberries

150 g (5 oz) blueberries

200 g (7 oz) strawberries, stalks removed

100 g (3¹/2 oz) grapes, seedless

125 g (4 oz/¹/2 cup) caster sugar

4 cloves

2 green cardamom pods

2.5 cm (1 in) piece of cinnamon stick

pinch of ground nutmeg (optional)

125 g (4 oz/1 cup) plain (all-purpose) white flour, sifted

100 g (3¹/2 oz) plain wholemeal flour

100 g (3¹/2 oz) unsalted butter

75g (3 oz/¹/2 cup) demerara sugar

50 g (2 oz/¹/3 cup) toasted hazelnuts roughly chopped

Place the fruits in a pan with about 2.5 cm (1 in) water. Add the caster sugar, cloves, green cardamom, cinnamon stick and nutmeg (if you are using it). Cook gently for 10–15 minutes or until the fruits are soft without being pulpy. Remove the whole spices and discard them.

In a bowl sift the white and wholemeal flour. Rub in the butter until the mixture resembles coarse breadcrumbs. Add the demerara sugar and the chopped hazelnuts. Mix well.

Butter a large baking dish and fill it with the fruit mixture. Pour half the juice in the dish and reserve the other half of the excess liquid for a coulis. Generously sprinkle over the crumble topping.

Bake in a preheated oven, at a moderate heat (200°C/400°F/gas 6) for 20–25 minutes, or until golden and crunchy.

Serve hot, drizzled with the remaining fruit coulis or with pouring cream.

AYURVEDA
healing from within

'Ayurveda' is known as the ancient science of life. It has been practised for generations in India and follows simple rules to help you live a long healthy life. The teachings of Ayurveda focus on the subtle energies that exist in all things. It is these energies that allow us to keep a health equilibrium and so avoid disease and illness.

Food sustains the body, and your diet plays an important role in how you are able to keep your body full of energy. All foods can be spread over three categories, or 'doshas', which help to balance and regulate the human body. It is believed that an imbalance of these doshas leads to disease.

All Indian spices, vegetables, pulses and grains have Ayurvedic properties that help keep the body healthy. Through the balance of these foods you can benefit from the Ayurvedic healing properties they possess.

These are a small collection of Ayurvedic recipes. Each one is unique and all carry specific attributes to help heal and balance the body and mind. I hope you too are able to benefit from the teachings of Ayurveda.

SWEET BANANA MILK
with hints of saffron
Zafarani kella ras

This recipe is great for giving you an early morning boost of energy. It helps you feel full of life and vitality. Ayurvedic medicine believes that milk naturally heals from within and if eaten as part of a balanced diet, can even prevent the signs of ageing. It helps to eliminate toxins in the body and so flushes out the bad bacteria that cause illness and disease. Bananas help to build bones and together with green cardamom, they strengthen the heart. Saffron has a special use of being the favoured spice for worship but in this recipe it is used for its calming effect on the nervous system. All these ingredients combined together help to elevate the soul and bring a wonderful glow to the skin.

serves four

8 bananas, peeled and chopped
600 ml (1 pint/2¹/₂ cups) milk
2 tablespoons sugar, to taste
2 saffron strands
2 green cardamom pods, ground (with husks)
fresh mint, to garnish

Mix all the ingredients in a food processor or blender until smooth and thick. Serve garnished with fresh mint.

'TEMPERED' black lentils

Tadka urad aur methi ki dal

Whole black lentils provide much-needed protein in the diet. They provide energy, as do fenugreek seeds. They have a heating effect and help to overcome weakness. Ginger and chilli combat coughs and colds, and coriander and cumin aid digestion. If turmeric does not kill the toxins in the body, then water will flush them out. This balanced dish provides internal balance and gives you essential energy.

serves four

200 g (7 oz/1 cup) whole black lentils, soaked overnight in water
2 tablespoons fenugreek seeds, soaked overnight in the water with the lentils
850 ml (1 pint 9 oz/4 cups) water
1 teaspoon fresh root ginger, finely chopped
4 tablespoons vegetable oil
1/2 teaspoon garlic, chopped
1 teaspoon black mustard seeds
2 green cardamom pods, crushed coarsely
1 green chilli, chopped (optional)
1/4 teaspoon ground turmeric
1 teaspoon ground coriander
1/2 teaspoon ground cumin
1/8 teaspoon asafoetida
1 teaspoon salt (to taste)
100 g (3 1/2 oz/3/4 cup) onions, sliced

Drain the lentils and fenugreek seeds.

Boil water in a pan and add the lentils, fenugreek seeds and ginger. Leave to cook for 1 hour or until soft.

Heat 2 tablespoons of oil in a pan and add the garlic and black mustard seeds. When they begin to crackle add the green cardamom pods and green chilli (if using). Add the cooked lentils after 1 minute.

Bring the dal to a simmer and add the ground turmeric, ground coriander, ground cumin, asafoetida and the salt. Leave simmering for 5 minutes.

In another pan heat the remaining oil and fry the sliced onions until they are golden brown. Drain on absorbent paper. Sprinkle over the cooked dal and serve piping hot with plain basmati rice.

leafy greens AND VEGETABLES

Rai palak phudina subzi

This is a recipe that helps the body function as it should. Leafy green vegetables such as watercress and spinach are high sources of fibre, which is essential for the intestines to work properly. Tomatoes and red chilli powder contain high amounts of Vitamin A, which fights against colds and increases longevity. Garlic is great for blood circulation and purifies the blood. Turmeric, which I like to call the 'wonder spice', is a natural antiseptic and can be said to cure almost anything, inside or out.

serves four

2 teaspoons vegetable oil
3/4 teaspoon black mustard seeds
2 cloves garlic, chopped
1/4 teaspoon fresh root ginger, grated
1/8 teaspoon ground turmeric
1/4 teaspoon red chilli powder
1/8 teaspoon asafoetida
450 g (1 lb) baby spinach leaves
100 g (3 1/2 oz) large leaf watercress, chopped
6 fresh mint leaves
50 g (2 oz/1/3 cup) tomatoes, chopped
3/4 teaspoon salt
1/4 teaspoon sugar

In a pan heat the oil and add the mustard seeds, garlic, ginger, ground turmeric, red chilli powder and asafoetida. When they begin to crackle add the spinach, watercress and mint. Add the remainder of the ingredients and cook for 10 minutes. Sprinkle in some water if the subzi begins to stick. Serve hot with warm naan breads or chapattis.

chickpeas with DILL

Chole dildar

This recipe helps to keep you well balanced and in good health. Tomatoes carry cancer fighting properties, as well as high levels of vitamin A (which helps fight against coughs and colds). Dill weed is a stimulant and aids digestion. Turmeric cures you from the inside, whilst garlic is known to stop premature ageing, and so protects you from the outside. Chickpeas are a natural source of protein and give you energy and strength.

serves four

2 tablespoons vegetable oil
1 teaspoon black mustard seeds
¹/₄ teaspoon cumin seeds
¹/₈ teaspoon asafoetida
650 g (1 lb 7 oz) tinned chickpeas, drained and rinsed
25 g (1 oz) dill weed, chopped
50 g (2 oz/¹/₃ cup) tomatoes, chopped
2 cloves garlic, chopped
225 ml (8 fl oz/1 cup) water
¹/₄ teaspoon red chilli powder
¹/₄ teaspoon ground turmeric
1 teaspoon ground garam masala (see page 14)
1 teaspoon fresh root ginger, grated
1 teaspoon salt
1 teaspoon coriander seeds, roasted and ground (see page 13)
1 tablespoon fresh coriander (cilantro), chopped

Heat the oil in a pan and add the mustard seeds. When they begin to crackle add the cumin seeds and asafoetida. After 1 minute add 450 g (1 lb) of the chickpeas, the dill weed, tomatoes and garlic. Coarsely crush the remaining chickpeas and add this to the mixture. Add the water, red

chilli powder, ground turmeric, garam masala, ginger and the salt. Bring to the boil and then lower the heat and cook for 10 minutes.

Just before serving sprinkle with roasted coriander powder and the chopped coriander (cilantro). Cover for 3 minutes to allow the aromas to penetrate. Serve hot with fresh naan bread.

GINGER tea

Adraki chai

This recipe can easily be incorporated into your daily diet. Ginger is wonderful for curing coughs and colds and also aids digestion. Milk is great for clearing out toxins and the green cardamom helps to cleanse the liver and throat.

serves four

600 ml (1 pint/2¹/₂ cups) water
³/₄ teaspoon fresh root ginger, grated
2 green cardamom pods, crushed
450 ml (16 fl oz/2 cups) milk
2¹/₂ teaspoons tea leaves (or 4 tea bags)
4 teaspoons sugar (or as desired)

Heat the water in a pan. When it begins to boil add the ginger and green cardamom pods. Leave to simmer for 2 minutes before adding the rest of the ingredients.

Bring to the boil and then turn off the heat. Allow the tea to infuse for a further 2 minutes before straining and serving. Drink piping hot.

mixed vegetable CHIPS

Different vegetables provide various healing properties, but they all provide vitamins and nutrients that are vital for our bodies to function. Adding red chilli powder and black pepper helps you keep your immune system healthy and the use of cumin and coriander aids digestion.

serves four

500 g (1 lb 2 oz) mixed vegetables, thinly sliced (such as potatoes, carrots, turnips, beetroot (beet) and sweet potatoes)
oil for deep-frying
1 teaspoon sesame seeds
1/2 teaspoon ground black pepper
1 tablespoon cumin seeds, roasted and ground (see page 13)
1 teaspoon coriander seeds, roasted and ground (see page 13)
1/4 teaspoon red chilli powder
1 teaspoon sugar
1/2 teaspoon salt
juice of 1/2 lime (optional)

Pat the sliced vegetables until dry.

Heat the oil to 190°C (375°F) and deep-fry the vegetables in batches. When they have turned a light golden brown, remove and leave to drain on absorbent paper.

Repeat this until all the vegetables have been fried.

Dry-roast the sesame seeds in a dry frying pan. Coarsely crush them with a pestle and mortar. Tip this into a bowl and add the black pepper, ground roasted cumin, ground roasted coriander, red chilli powder, sugar and salt.

Sprinkle this spice mixture over the vegetable chips. Squeeze over the lime juice (if using) and serve. These can be kept in an airtight container for up to 2 weeks.

spicy SUNFLOWER SEEDS

Seeds are wonderfully nutritious and are a great energy booster. The presence of salt not only helps to give this dish a more balanced flavour, but it is believed that salt helps the growth and development of tissues. Together with asafoetida, salt is necessary for building physical strength and stamina. Coriander seeds are added to strengthen the body and soothe the heart. Ayurveda believes that cumin and black pepper help to cure coughs and aid digestion.

serves four

200 g (7 oz) sunflower seeds (unsalted)
1 tablespoon ghee or vegetable oil
1 teaspoon coriander seeds, roasted and ground (see page 13)
1/2 teaspoon cumin seeds, roasted and ground (see page 13)
1/2 teaspoon ground black pepper
1/4 teaspoon salt
1/8 teaspoon sugar
pinch of asafoetida (optional)
pinch of red chilli powder (optional)

Dry-roast the sunflower seeds in a dry frying pan for 5 minutes. Keep them moving around so that they brown evenly on all sides. Transfer to a bowl.

Heat the ghee or vegetable oil until warm and pour over the seeds.

Mix the remaining ingredients together and toss the seeds in the spice mixture.

Serve these warm or keep them in an airtight container for up to 2 weeks.

INDEX

anytime Indian omelette 32
aubergine with chives, smoked 106
aubergine and new potato curry 76

banana milk, sweet, with hints of saffron 122
banarasi pilau 80
bay beef salad 24
beans on toast, irresistible spiced 26
beef:
    bay beef salad 24
    chargrilled steak sandwich 41
    east-west burgers 22
bhajias, caramelised onion 30
bhendi: paneer and okra curry 82
biryani, the emperor's 96
Bombay pitta pockets 38
breads:
    Indian flat bread 16
    Indian puffed bread 17
    onion and coriander paratha 101
    spiced puri 90
broth, chicken and lentil 33
burgers, east-west 22

cachumbar, the ultimate snack with 40
caramelised onion bhajias 30
carpaccio, mango 114
cashews, chicken with 70 spiced 30
chargrilled steak sandwich 41
chicken:
    chicken with cashews 70
    chicken and lentil broth 33
    chicken tikka caesar salad 44
    chilli chicken wrap 40
    Kashmiri chilli chicken wings 25
    raj korma 85

slow-cooked chicken with smoked cumin 68
    tandoori chicken summer salad 54
chickpeas:
    chickpeas with dill 124
    princess salad 84
chilli chicken wrap 40
chilli, garlic and ginger paste 12
chips, mixed vegetable 125
chocolate pudding, molten 112
chutney, tomato 92
cilantro:
    fresh coriander and mint dip 15
    onion and coriander paratha 101
cinnamon crème brûlée 116
classic Indian tea 17
classic lassi 114
cod, laced coconut 67
coffee,
    iced cardamom 118
    slumber 17
corn-on-the-cob, Meena's 32
courgette prawns, hot and spicy 65
creamy vanilla rice pudding 107
crème brûlée, cinnamon 116
crispy spicy fish fillets 62
crumble, summer fruits crunchy 121

dals:
    tadka 93
    whole green 'tempered' lentil 88
dhansak, lamb 74
dips:
    fresh coriander and mint 15
    fruity tamarind and date 15
    garlic lovers' 15
drinks:
    classic Indian tea 17

classic lassi 114
ginger tea 124
iced cardamom coffee 118
slumber coffee 17
summer cooler 119
sweet banana milk with hints of saffron 122

east-west burgers 22
eggplants:
    aubergine and new potato curry 76
    smoked aubergines with chives 106
emperor's biryani 96

fish:
    crispy spicy fish fillets 62
    Goan fish curry 63
    Hyderabadi fish curry 66
    laced coconut cod 67
    south Indian steamed monkfish parcels 53
    spicy chilli fish cakes 21
    tandoori crusted salmon 50
fresh coriander and mint dip 15
fresh vegetable samosas 29
fruits, grilled aromatic 57
fruity tamarind and date dip 15

garam masala, Meena's 14
garlic lover's dip 15
ginger tea 124
Goan fish curry 63
grilled aromatic fruits 57

hot and spicy courgette prawns 65
Hyderabadi fish curry 66

iced cardamom coffee 118
Indian flat bread 16
Indian puffed bread 17
irresistible spiced beans on toast 26

jalebis 108

Kashmiri chilli chicken wings 25
kebabs, spicy lamb 51
korma, raj 85

laced coconut cod 67
lamb:
    Emperor's biryani 96
    lamb dhansak 74
    lamb shakuti 69
    lamb shank rogan josh 73
    slow roast lamb 104
    spicy lamb kebabs 51
lassi, classic 114
leafy greens and vegetables 123
lentils:
    lentils with cream and butter 81
    south Indian lentil curry 89
    tadka dal 93
    'tempered' black lentils 123
    whole green 'tempered' lentil dal 88
light tomato soup with baby spinach 100

mango carpaccio 114
mango and chilli sorbet 117
mango-glazed pork chops 47
masala, pan-fried potato 78
Meena's chilli ginger mussels 20
Meena's corn-on-the-cob 32
Meena's garam masala 14
mini stuffed jackets 46
mixed vegetable chips 125
molten chocolate pudding 112
monkfish parcels, south Indian steamed 53
mussels, Meena's chilli ginger 20

okra curry, paneer and 82
omelette, anytime Indian 32

onion bhajias, caramelised 30
onion and coriander paratha
  101

pan-fried potato masala 78
paneer and okra curry 82
paneer tikka 79
panini, roasted tikka vegetable
  48
paratha, onion and coriander
  101
pilau, banarasi 80
pineapple pudhina 118
pitta pockets, Bombay 38
pork:
  mango-glazed pork chops
    47
  pork sorpotel 75
  spicy sticky spare ribs 23
potato:
  aubergine and new potato
    curry 76
  mini stuffed jackets 46
  pan-fried potato masala 78
  potato and yoghurt curry 77
  potatoes stuffed with green
    peas 35
  tikka potato wedges and
    dip 26
prawns:
  hot and spicy courgette
    prawns 65
  seared Keralan prawns 39
  sesame battered tikka
    prawns 61
  spicy prawn salad 64
princess salad 84
puri, spiced 90

raj korma 85
rice:
  banarasi pilau 80
  boiled basmati rice 14
  emperor's biryani 96
  rice pudding, creamy
    vanilla 107
  wilted spinach and tomato
    rice 98
  roasted tikka vegetable
    panini 48
rogan josh, lamb shank 73

saffron semolina pudding 119
salads:
  bay beef 24
  chicken tikka caesar 44
  princess 84
  spicy prawn 64
  tandoori chicken
    summer 54
  salmon, tandoori crusted 50
  samosas, fresh vegetable 29
sandwich, chargrilled steak 41
sauce bases:
  sautéed onion 13
  spicy tomato curry 13
sautéed onion sauce base 13
seafood caldin 60
seared Keralan prawns 39
semolina pudding, saffron 119
sesame battered tikka prawns
  61
short-eats 47
shrimp:
  hot and spicy courgette
    prawns 65
  seared Keralan prawns 39
  sesame battered tikka
    prawns 61
  spicy prawn salad 64
slow-cooked chicken with
  smoked cumin 68
slow roast lamb 104
slumber coffee 17
smoked aubergine with chives
  106
smoky sweet potatoes 51
sorbet, mango and chilli 117
sorpotel, pork 75
soup, light tomato, with baby
  spinach 100
south Indian lentil curry 89
south Indian steamed
  monkfish parcels 53
spare ribs, sticky spicy 23
spiced cashews 30
spiced puri 90
spiced tomato curry base 13
spiced vegetable medley 91
spices,
  roasted 13
  to temper 12
spicy chilli fish cakes 21

spicy lamb kebabs 51
spicy prawn salad 64
spicy sticky spare ribs 23
spicy sunflower seeds 125
summer cooler 119
summer fruits crunchy
  crumble 121
sunflower seeds, spicy 125
sweet banana milk with hints
  of saffron 122
sweet potatoes, smoky 51

tadka dal 93
tandoori chicken summer
  salad 54
tandoori crusted salmon 50
tea, classic Indian 17
  ginger 124
'tempered' black lentils 123
tikka, paneer 79
tikka potato wedges and dip
  26
tomato chutney 92
tomato soup, light, with baby
  spinach 100

ultimate snack with
  cachumbar 40

vegetables:
  fresh vegetable samosas 29
  leafy greens and vegetables
    123
  mixed vegetable chips 125
  roasted tikka vegetable
    panini 48
  spiced vegetable medley 91
vegetarian dishes:
  anytime Indian omelette 32
  aubergine and new potato
    curry 76
  Bombay pitta pockets 38
  cachumbar 40
  caramelised onion bhajias
    30
  chickpeas with dill 124
  fresh vegetable samosas 29
  irresistible spiced beans on
    toast 26
  leafy greens and vegetables
    123

lentils with cream and
  butter 81
light tomato soup with
  baby spinach 100
Meena's corn-on-the-cob 32
mini stuffed jackets 46
mixed vegetable chips 125
pan-fried potato masala 78
paneer and okra curry 82
paneer tikka 79
potato and yoghurt curry 77
potatoes stuffed with green
  peas 35
princess salad 84
roasted tikka vegetable
  panini 48
short-eats 47
smoked aubergines with
  chives 106
smoky sweet potatoes 51
south Indian lentil curry 89
spiced cashews 30
spiced vegetable medley 91
spicy sunflower seeds 125
tadka dal 93
'tempered' black lentils 123
tikka potato wedges and
  dip 26

whole green 'tempered' lentil
  dal 88
wilted spinach and tomato
  rice 98
wrap, chilli chicken 40

zucchini:
  hot and spicy courgette
    prawns 65

ACKNOWLEDGEMENTS

Very special thanks to my daughter Anjali who has worked meticulously hard and has put endless hours into helping me complete this book on time. I could not have achieved this mammoth task without her at such a very busy point in my life.

Also to Debbie Thomas who has put all her passion and time into making this book come to reality with her innovative ideas.

To Vijay Anand, our Development Chef who helped Anjali and I bring the recipes to life.

To Clare Sayer and Rosemary Wilkinson at New Holland who have once again had the patience and belief in me to write another book.

To the photographer Stuart West for his excellent photographs.

Also to Eliza Baird for her wonderful food styling.

To Violet Bell for typing up the recipes.

To my sons Neeraj and Nayan and the team at Patak's for testing out the recipes and for giving such helpful feedback.

Last but not least, my husband Kirit for always being by my side and encouraging me throughout my life in all my endeavours and for having the vision to lead Patak's into the third generation.